We Are the Question + the Answer

Break the Collective Habit of Racism + Build Resilience for Racial Equity in Ourselves and Our Organizations

Dr. S. Atyia Martin, CEM

All Aces Publishing

Boston

- ➲ **LinkedIn**: https://www.linkedin.com/company/all-aces-inc/
- ➲ **Facebook**: https://www.facebook.com/allacesboston
- ➲ **Twitter**: https://twitter.com/allaces_inc
- ➲ **Instagram**: https://www.instagram.com/allacesboston/

ISBN: 978-1-7364180-0-0

DEDICATION

To my family…I love you with all that I am. Never forget: Last name first. To my mentors, friends, and colleagues over the years that I have learned so much from. To those people I may never meet who are striving to improve themselves and this world while recognizing the relationship between the two.

TABLE OF CONTENTS

FIGURES/GRAPHICS

TABLES

INTRODUCTION

This book comes from a place of research, experience, humanity, humility, hope, and love.

Growing up, I used to be exhaustingly angry at White People.

I did not understand how they did not understand. As a Black, African American child, I could not wrap my mind around their obliviousness to the pain, frustration, humiliation, dehumanization, and ultimately, the indignities that were regularly directed at me and other Black People.

To me, the evidence of racism was everywhere. Look at the uncritically accepted ideas about who I am based solely on me being Black. As if only White People had a right to be an individual, to have success, to be smart, or to be treated as fully human. Look at the disinvestment in my community. As if the only determination of my community's struggles rested with individual effort, regardless of the historically documented laws, policies, and behavior (by individuals and organizations) that most people never learn in school. Or worse, as if the challenges for my community derived from some defect with our "culture."

It was not until I was an adult that I began to unravel the complicated truth of the matter: Most White People really did not understand. It was not their experience. How could I expect them to understand something for which they had no frame of reference? Most White People do not really know People of Color. I do not mean the superficial interactions that still leave plenty of room to view us as the stereotypes that mask our full humanity. History, social standards, incentivization, power, conformity, and comfort all align and conspire in a system that has become self-sustaining. The system upholds whiteness (the concept not White People) as the bar of *normalcy* against which everyone should be measured. The perch of normalcy from which most White People view the world makes me as a whole person and the experiences of other People of Color invisible. Whiteness disguised as normalcy also makes White People blind to their complicity in the hustle of racism. Finally, it makes them blind to their own pain and suffering in their other role as part of the hustled masses. The invisible hand of racism touches all of us.

Because that invisible hand is indiscriminate, I have also witnessed people who look like me uncritically accept whiteness as the bar of normalcy. People of Color who think that they were an exception to the rules. The rules that say People of Color are less than, flawed, and undeserving. Therefore, we should all be convinced that our pain and experiences are the "normal" consequence of our deficits. And anyone who is not a stereotype is special, different, exempt from the burden of society that the rest of us deserve to shoulder. The rules that say we were destined for poverty, mediocrity, and insecurity. The rules that demand our *gratitude* to be in certain spaces, in spite of our hard-fought battles to get there. That insist we be superhuman so we can "pull ourselves up by our bootstraps." That withhold dignity or the benefit of the doubt...that is reserved for White People. There are many People of Color for whom these untruths are not self-evident. Perhaps they know it intellectually, but social conditioning is real.

The foundational ideas of racism are readily internalized with the insurmountable amount of information, symbols, media, and people in our lives reinforcing these ideas. So, it comes as no surprise that there are People of Color who have benefited from racism as unhealthy gatekeepers: The defenders of the undefendable. People of Color are on the same treadmill as our White brothers and sisters where whiteness is both the carrot and the stick. The benefits require us to sacrifice any hopes of self-determination and human growth and development. Accepting the conformity of whiteness (usually an unconscious process, but not always), offers crumbs to keep us chasing. We hold on to these crumbs for dear life. While those who work diligently to *not* internalize and accept whiteness are deemed abnormal, defective, or weird; ostracized and crumb-less. The crumbs are from a much larger gourmet meal that an exclusive number of people get to enjoy.

In the cases of People of Color and White People, a habit of racism has been developed across generations. The habit has been cultivated not only as individual, but one that is cultural and systemic...collective. The habit is embedded in our ideas, how we see ourselves, how we see others, the way we structure and run organizations, and where we do and do not place value. However, it does not have to be this way.

We are the Question + the Answer, as a title, acknowledges that we are still struggling so deeply with racism because we do not see ourselves as part of the problem or the solution. Many of us talk about dismantling the system of racism, but we are all part of the system we are trying to change. Changing the system means changing ourselves. Each of us can opt out of being passive conductors of racism and oppression and opt in to being proactive disruptors.

This book was born out of sadness and hope. Sadness that most of us do not take personal responsibility for our individual role in the system of racism. People and organizations have rendered themselves as *bystanders* to racism despite our overt and covert behavior that stealthily and steadily fuels it. We seem to not be able to dismount the treadmill of racial oppression. It is comforting in its rhythmic predictability, structure, and expectations--even though many of us at least suspect that there must be more to life, to ourselves, and to each other.

However, I have tremendous hope. Hope in our desire to truly be connected to others and something bigger than ourselves. Hope in our ability to evolve our understanding; to grow and learn. I find it fascinating that we have an exponentially higher level of thinking and innovation than any other living being on earth. This is an opportunity because many of us are not tapping into our full capabilities of learning and adaptation: We are not building or using our resilience. We are not realizing our full human potential if we are on the treadmill of racism. With every step, it feels like we are making progress (and in some limited ways, we are), but we have not covered any transformational ground because we have not transformed ourselves. Those who have taken on the pursuit of freedom know that freedom is not free. We all need to know that freedom is not free. To free ourselves from the subliminal comfort of racism means that we have to explore the untouched wilderness: Who are you? What do you *really* want? What do you *really* believe? Why? To be free means a level of responsibility and commitment that places the onus on us. We have to create our own definitions of success, relationships, organizational culture, and ourselves.

I wrote the following reflection to myself while participating in a diversity training after President Trump was elected:

"*Journal on Trump Election*

I do not fear Trump taking office in the same way others do. I am concerned about the impact of his presidency on those who are outcasted from society and/or dependent on government programs from the federal level. After the election, I was more emboldened in doing racial equity and social justice work. I have made this commitment professionally and personally.

"Professionally, I am in a position that is explicitly focused on this issue. However, because I do not have final say on the direction, I have to channel my unused thoughts, energy, and expertise to my personal efforts. I am shifting to doing more consulting, training, and workshops to help my personal philosophy of individual and institutional responsibility for confronting racism and advancing racial equity.

"My hope is that others feel the urgency of what was revealed about the hearts, minds, and challenges of working-class White Americans...that others will also be more emboldened. That there is an exploration of how racism hurts White People and how they are being deceived. This is an opportunity to change the narrative: about the connections of the struggle, the institutional and structural issues...

"Life is 10% what happens to us and 90% how we respond."

"Thou shall not be a victim. Thou shall not be a perpetrator. But above all thou shall not be a bystander.""

This note to myself turned into me leaving my position as Chief Resilience Officer for the City of Boston to focusing full time on my business, All Aces, Inc. I continued to revisit resources that provided context on what racism is, how it works, how it impacts us as individuals and in organizations, and approaches to address it from the social justice and racism-specific literature (books, reports, peer-reviewed articles, videos, etc.). Over the years, I have felt like many of these resources were missing major pieces of the puzzle, but I could not put my finger on them. However, I did notice that racism seemed to exist at the intersection of neuroscience, sociology, and psychology. I read about implicit bias; critical thinking; habit formation and change; individual, organizational, and community trauma; human and organizational development; cognitive behavioral therapy; behavioral economics; leadership; and more.

I began to develop language for what was missing from the traditional conversations on racism. We were talking about racism in ways that:

- ⮞ Focus on the benefits to, challenges for, and needs of White People;
- ⮞ Reduce People of Color to participants and props for the learning of White People;
- ⮞ Applies oversimplified framing that People of Color are victims and White People are perpetrators;
- ⮞ Strip away the complexity of how People of Color can be complicit as conductors of racism and oppression to the detriment of ourselves and other People of Color;
- ⮞ Overintellectualize racism to be about definitions, the "right words," and policing what other people say;
- ⮞ Lacks practical approaches that help to build skills and apply tools for each layer of racism: ideological, internalized, interpersonal, and institutional (see Chapter 1 for more information on the layers of racism).

Going into all of these different rabbit holes of knowledge has not only been about an exploration to develop approaches for my work or business. It has also been a journey for me to deepen my own practice and increase my personal effectiveness in being a disruptor of oppression in myself, my family, and the organizations that are important in my life. What I soon discovered was that many of the approaches, strategies, and tactics to confronting racism and advancing racial equity that have been beneficial to me and All Aces' clients, are the same things we needed to be doing to be better people and organizations…to reach our full potential.

This book is not THE answer; it is a reframing for what we think we already know about confronting racism and advancing racial equity. It is my contribution based on what I have personally researched and experienced in practice with people and organizations. It is not a book of definitions or a detailed analysis of everything racism. It is my attempt to synthesize the most important lessons I have learned on my journey. I included many of the original sources that helped me to think differently about this work in case you want to go deeper.

As you read and reflect on *We Are the Question + the Answer*, I also hope you sense all of the intentional efforts to take a developmental approach to helping people and organizations to **ACT:** (1) **A**ctivate consciousness and reframing racism, how it works as an individual and collective set of habits, and how it impacts all of us; (2) **C**atalyze critical thinking to analyze and break the habits of racism; and (3) **T**ransform our individual and collective capabilities to advance racial equity as a new, intentional habit. I also hope that you join our learning community, **IntentionallyAct.com**, to continue to learn and be connected to others who are professionally and personally committed to doing the same.

I recognize that not everyone is ready. I am not sure I am, but I know that if I always waited until I was, I would have never taken advantage of opportunities that were outside my comfort zone. If we waited until we were *ready* for everything, nothing would get done. The progress and healing we need is in the doing. We have to act and do it now. In most movements, there are a small number of people who catalyze and facilitate the majority of the work and bring others along on the journey. As someone who is reading this book, I welcome you to the work and journey with open arms and love.

1. THE HABIT OF RACISM

"Sow a thought and you reap an action; sow an act and you reap a habit; sow a habit and you reap a character; sow a character and you reap a destiny."
– Ralph Waldo Emerson

We have been destined for racial and social injustice because we have sowed racist thoughts that have led to racist actions that are now unquestioned racist habits. I rarely use the word racist to describe individuals because most of us have been taught the habits of racism. However, I am using the word racist to describe our habitual thinking and behavior that reinforce racism.

Habit: "A settled tendency or usual manner of behavior; addiction; an acquired mode of behavior that has become nearly or completely involuntary; a behavior pattern acquired by frequent repetition or physiologic exposure that shows itself in regularity or increased facility of performance."[1]

Racism is a habit. It is an individual, institutional, and structural habit, which is why it is systemic (we will cover this shortly). Habits are formed by repetitive exposure to mutually reinforcing communication, thinking, and behavior. Oftentimes, habit creation and its impacts are left hidden to us. "When a habit emerges, the brain stops fully participating in decision making."[2] Therefore, unless we fight a habit, the pattern will unfold automatically, invisible to us.

Let's break down the definition of habit:

- ➲ A settled tendency or usual manner of behavior: This part of the definition speaks to how racism presents itself. The ideas that comprise the ideology of racism have become so baked into our society and culture they are invisible to us. We think of negative outcomes for People of Color as expected and struggling White People as an anomaly. It is a vicious cycle: Our behavior is driven by these flawed ideas and our behavior reinforces them.

- ➲ <u>Addiction</u>: a psychological and physical inability to stop consuming a chemical, drug, ***activity***, or substance, even though it is causing psychological and physical harm. Racism is an activity that causes tremendous psychological and physical harm to People of Color. What is not often discussed is that it also causes psychological and physical harm to White People. Ultimately, the habits of racism have been a form of instinctual addiction to the concepts of normalcy and conformity.

- ➲ <u>An acquired mode of behavior that has become nearly or completely involuntary</u>: We have been so overexposed to ideas about People of Color as inferior and powerless and White People as superior and powerful that we have internalized these ideas whether we consciously believe them or not. The internalization facilitates habitual behavior in our interactions with each other and how organizations operate.

- ➲ <u>A behavior pattern acquired by frequent repetition or physiologic exposure that shows itself in regularity or increased facility of performance</u>: Racism is a discernable pattern of behavior in people and institutions that has become easier for us to engage in over time…so easy that, for the most part, we do not realize that each of us has become a cog in the machine of racism…we are part of the system. The internalization of constant exposure to ideas, behavior, and policies that support racism is what catalyzes the illogical behaviors that we exhibit.

Racism has become such a habit that people who have bought in to the concept of whiteness are painfully predictable in their psychologically violent response when exposed to mountains of evidence about racism's realities, from fields such as history, neuroscience, psychology, sociology, etc. Proof is unable to conquer the deep-seeded beliefs that our society constantly waters. Contrary to our self-delusions, we are not rational beings. We are not wired to analyze information, question our thinking and behavior, and change our position or behavior based on the outcome. We are not taught how to apply a process that helps us manage this reality so we can analyze and address the nuances of racism.

To apply such a process requires a combination of interrelated skills: racial equity literacy, emotional intelligence, critical thinking, communication, and conflict management. We have taken our ability to perform these skills for granted. We think that we perform these skills well. However, if there has been no effort to learn, practice, and apply them in everyday situations, then the chances are slim to none that we are doing them well—or at all. In other words, if it does not feel like we are exerting any effort when we are interacting with ourselves and others or making decisions then we are not deploying these skills.

Furthermore, many of us do not actually understand ourselves. We do not understand human behavior, how our own behavior is influenced by external forces, or how to have a real relationship with ourselves and others. At a basic level, many of us do not comprehend why we believe what we believe or do what we do. When is the last time you analyzed your own behavior or decision-making process?

Eduardo Bonilla-Silva described the concept of racism without racists in his book of the same title. It speaks to the subtle, non-race explicit ways that racism manifests itself on a regular basis, as well as the wide participation of mostly unsuspecting White People.[3] In essence, he is describing a systemic habit. However, I would add it also includes the wide participation of mostly unsuspecting Black, Indigenous, and People of Color (BIPOC). Frederick Douglass said:

> "Power concedes nothing without a demand. It never did and it never will. Find out just what any people will quietly submit to and you have found out the exact measure of injustice and wrong which will be imposed upon them, and these will continue till they are resisted…"

Frederick Douglass speaks to the complicity the oppressed can play in reinforcing the very systems that cause us harm. If we, BIPOC, play a role in the system of racism, then we also need to develop our knowledge, skills, and tools to advocate for ourselves and others. I also extend this concept to White People, who are playing a dual role as the oppressed and benefitting from oppression. I had to come to terms with my own well-watered seeds of racism that had blossomed in every aspect of my life. It took me quite a bit of time to realize that it was not just White People who were upholding the system of racism. I am a part of the same ecosystem…I experience the pain and suffering from racism. I also think and behave in habitual ways that nurture it. I could not shift the dynamics of that ecosystem without shifting myself and my habits.

Bonilla-Silva's concept of racism without racists is similar to Hannah Arendt's description of tyranny without a tyrant. It is a Kafkaesque perspective that the seemingly inexplicable momentum of some systems can seem unstoppable even by supposedly powerful people. The system's original catalyst and desired outcomes transform into a series of nonsensical logic that begins to perpetuate itself into unconscious habits that we no longer question. We just do what we have been doing because that is the way we always have – this is how the habit of racism works. However, by fine-tuning our attention to the hypocrisy and habits of racism, we can see our shortcomings and pivot. We live in a world that we shape and sustain. Therefore, we have the power to change it.

What are our racism-reinforcing habits? How do we change them? There are a number of frameworks and approaches to understanding habits that can be applied to help answer these questions. I appreciate the simplicity of Charles Duhigg's book *The Power of Habit: Why We Do What We Do in Life and Business*. Synthesizing a large amount of research and context into a manageable framework, Duhigg proposes a habit loop (cue-craving-routine-reward) in understanding and changing our habits. "New habits are created: by putting together a cue, a routine, a reward, and then cultivating a craving that drives the loop."[2]

From a habit change perspective, I appreciate James Clear's book *Atomic Habits: An Easy & Proven Way to Build Good Habits & Break Bad Ones*. "Many people walk through life in a cognitive slumber, blindly following the norms attached to their identity…The more deeply a thought or action is tied to your identity, the more difficult it is to change it…true behavior change, is identity change…"[4] We have the power to reimagine our identity and create new racial equity reinforcing habits. This book is meant to support that process.

With racism, the craving for whiteness (as a concept) has become the model of normalcy that all of us should strive to attain. This craving has been cultivated in us since we were born and as far back as before the United States was officially a country. Although whiteness is the craving that drives the habits of racism, what we are really chasing are the rewards that are promised to those who conform to it. However, the rewards of whiteness can become magnified to fool people into thinking the crumbs they are eating are an actual meal. Take for example the words of an Eastern Virginia slaveholder, who pointed out that in his part of the state more than half the white people had "little but their complexion to console them for being born into a higher caste."[5]

What is a craving and where does it come from? A craving is an overwhelming emotional experience that represents a specific manifestation of a deeper underlying motive—the reward we are subliminally seeking. Of the many models for human motivation, I chose Maslow's Hierarchy of Needs for its depth, breadth, and simplicity.[6, 7] Maslow initially stated that individuals must satisfy lower-level deficit needs before progressing on to meet higher level growth needs. However, he later clarified that the satisfaction of a need is not an "all-or-none" phenomenon, admitting that his earlier statements may have given "the false impression that a need must be satisfied 100 percent before the next need emerges."[8] In other words, it is quite possible to reach our growth needs even if the basic needs are not fully met. The following is a brief overview of each level of Maslow's Hierarchy:

➲ **Physiological Needs [Deficiency Need]**: Breathing, Water, Food, Shelter, Clothing, Sleep;

➲ **Safety & Security [Deficiency Need]**: Health, Property, Family,

Stability. protection from elements, security, order, law, stability, freedom from fear;

- **Love & Belonging [Deficiency Need]**: Friendship, Family, Intimacy, Sense of Connection. The need for interpersonal relationships motivates our behavior.
- **Esteem [Deficiency Need]**: Confidence, Mastery, Achievement, Respect of Others. Esteem for ourselves and the desire for the respect of others, which Maslow believed preceded real self-esteem or dignity.
- **Self-Actualization [Growth Need]**: Morality, Creativity, Spontaneity, Acceptance, Purpose. Self-actualization is a continual process of becoming who we can be rather than a final destination.
- **Self-Transcendence [Growth Need]**: Sensemaking, Meaning of Life, Oneness, Worldview, Power of Mind, Flux, Transformation, Interdependence (Maslow added this need later).[7]

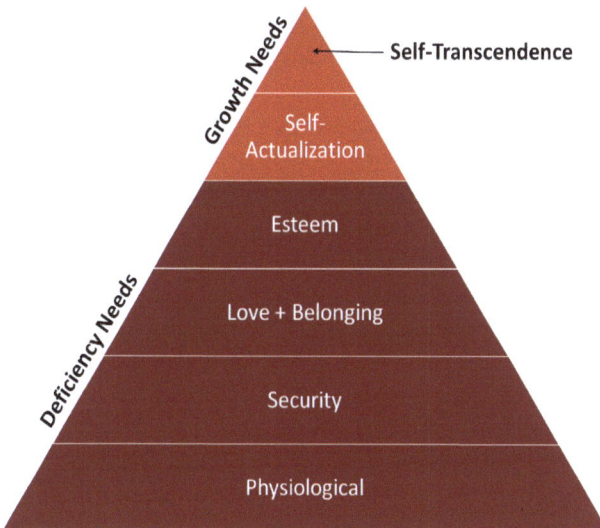

Figure 1: Maslow's Hierarchy of Needs

The deficiency needs of Maslow's Hierarchy result from deprivation and tends to motivate people when they are unmet. However, motivation decreases as these needs are met. This is why in dysfunctional organizations, perks and bonuses by themselves are not enough to keep employees (or keep them engaged) over time. People are looking to meet their growth needs which requires an intentional culture that is not based on carrots and sticks, but growth and development.[9] Growth needs do not come from a lack of something, but rather from a desire to reach our full potential in our lives and organizations; these needs continue to be felt and may even become stronger once they have been engaged.[10]

The rewards of engaging in the habits of racism are based on deficiency needs. We gain a sense of comfort and acceptance by conforming to the ideas, self-perception, interactions, and organizational culture that come with oppression. We can show up and go along with the program without having to figure anything out for ourselves. We trade our power in exchange for the external validation and motivation of deficiency needs. The ideas, symbols, signs, words, and behaviors of racism act as cues for the expectations associated with whiteness and antiblackness. When we walk into an organization and there are only pictures of White People. When we sit in the lunchroom and the conversations indicate it is acceptable to make jokes about other people's race. When we are in a meeting and the leadership asks for feedback, but upon receiving concerns about issues related to racism is dismissive or accusatory.

These cues trigger a craving for whiteness that has been taught covertly to us and drives our conformity to its standards of normalcy so we can get rewarded by having our underlying needs met. This craving then triggers thought and behavioral routines that reinforce racism. There are times we make a conscious decision to conform, but most of the time we are unconsciously participating in routines to get these rewards. The biggest rewards for our compliance come from our jobs. We have to feed our families and for many of us, our work is a major part of our identity. When we see ourselves as being what we do, there are even more incentives to comply.

Rewards are powerful because they satisfy cravings. But we are often not conscious of the cravings that drive our behaviors. Most cravings are obvious in retrospect, but incredibly hard to see when we are under their influence. We will allow our own dignity to be violated and violate others' dignity to gain safety and security, love and belonging, self-esteem, acceptance, and to be a part of something that seems bigger than ourselves. (See *The Habit of Racism* figure on the next page for a visual overview.)

When considering the way Maslow's Hierarchy also aligns with other models that focus on human development, like Kohlberg's Moral Stages or Loevinger's Model of Ego Development, it reinforces my belief that our ability to reach our full human potential requires us to increase: (1) the complexity of our thinking, (2) our knowledge and management of self, and (3) respect for our interdependence with each other and the world around us.

Normalcy/Whiteness

Craving

Cues

⊃ Environment
⊃ Urgency/Time
⊃ Emotional State
⊃ Other People
⊃ Activating Situation

The Habit of Racism

Response/ Routines

Ideological +
Internalized +
Interpersonal +
Institutional Racism-
Reinforcing Habits

Rewards

⊃ Physiological
⊃ Safety/Security
⊃ Love/Belonging
⊃ Esteem

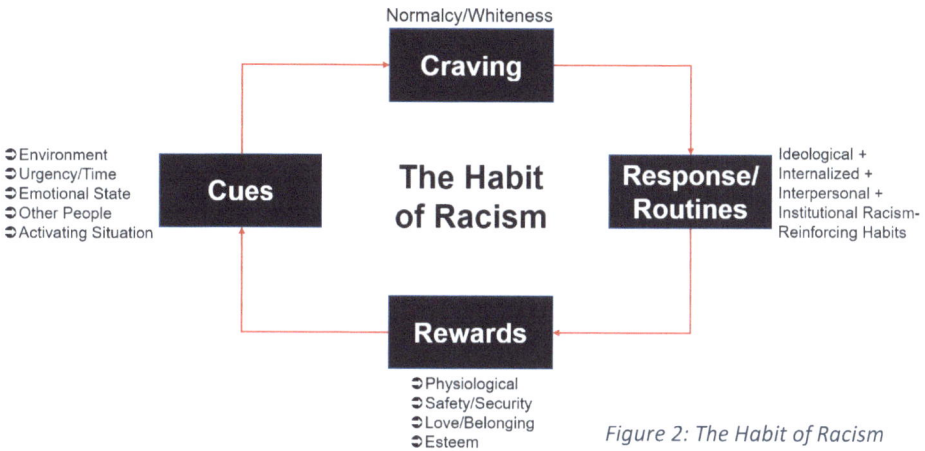

Figure 2: The Habit of Racism

These models are relevant because they show the potential return on investment of prioritizing our own development to reduce the underlying motivations for our racism reinforcing behaviors. This investment is our best offense for, and defense against, the thinking and behaviors that are detrimental to ourselves and each other. Focusing on growth-based rewards, self-actualization and self-transcendence, means we are internally driven instead of being driven by or trying to drive people with unfulfilling, oppressive carrots and sticks. Ultimately, our commitment to advancing racial equity is a journey to rehumanize ourselves and others by breaking these mindless cycles and learning how to be our best selves, especially when times are hard.

There are many theories of human and cognitive development that you can choose to learn. Researchers have aligned these models to show their parallels, from Robert Kegan's Constructive Developmental Theory (CDT) (also referred to as the Five Stages of Development) to Jane Loevinger's Stages of Ego Development.[11] I have aligned these two approaches to thinking about our human development with Maslow's Hierarchy to show how the underlying motivations of our behavior evolve to focus on growth needs. Additionally, it helps us understand the human development foundations that racism is built upon. There are also parallels with the various models for the stages of racial identity development from thought leaders like Bailey W. Jackson, Jean Kim, Rita Hardiman, and Janet Helms.[12, 13] These models were significantly informed by cognitive development research. Although the stages fit neatly into the table below, reality is a bit messier. You can ebb and flow across all of these stages over the course of a day. However, what matters is how we manage ourselves to spend most of our time at the higher end of the spectrum…closer to our better selves.

Level	Maslow's Hierarchy of Needs	Stages of Adult Development	Stages of Ego Development
1	Physiological Needs	Impulsive Mind	E1: Symbiotic E2: Impulsive
2	Safety Need	Instrumental Mind	E3: Self-Protective
3	Love & Belonging	Socialized Mind	E4: Conformist
4	Esteem Self-Actualization	Self-Authoring Mind	E5: Self-Aware E6: Conscientious
5	Self-Transcendence	Self-Transforming Mind	E7: Individualist E8: Autonomous E9: Integrated

Figure 3: Alignment of Maslow's Hierarchy with Cognitive and Ego Development

Level 1. We are driven by having our basic physiological needs met. Our mental complexity is at its lowest level. We live in an objectless world where everything is taken to be an extension of ourselves. We cannot determine the boundaries between ourselves and the environment. This is where most infants are. We are ego-centric and dependent in how we engage with others. Although this is a place where infants spend most of their development, we as adults can find ourselves here when we are in survival mode.

Level 2. We seek security through order and law. We understand blame, but we externalize it to other people or to circumstances. Morality to us is essentially a matter of anticipating rewards and punishments (think of Maslow's deficiency needs). We develop meaning making, realize that we have control over our reflexes, and become aware of objects in our environment as independent from ourselves. However, our thinking tends to be imaginative and illogical, our feelings impulsive and fluid, and self-centered in our interactions with others. At this level, we crave a morally prescribed, rigidly enforced, unchanging order. If maintained too long, an older child or adult who remains here may become opportunistic, deceptive, and preoccupied with control.

Level 3. We are driven by our need to be affiliated with a group. We seek esteem through recognition or achievement from others. This is the level mo st adults are. We are shaped by the definitions and expectations of our personal environment. Who we think we are is based on our connection with, and loyalty to, the identities and groups with which we align ourselves. Our sense of self can express itself primarily in our relationships with other people, with schools of thought (ideas and beliefs of groups) or both. I am also flagging the danger of Level 3: It facilitates groupthink which is rampant in most of our lives and organizations. Groupthink is a psychological phenomenon in which the desire for conformity in a group results in dysfunctional decision-making outcomes.

An ability to understand rules of the group appears. A group member's disapproval becomes a sanction in and of itself, in addition to the fear of punishment. While in the role of the conformist, we like and trust other people within our own group. We may define that group narrowly and reject any or all outgroups, and stereotype roles on the principle of social desirability: When people are not like us, they are by default undesirable.[14, 15] Then we layer the social infection of ideas and habits that reinforce racism. It distinguishes race as defined groups that we belong to and therefore determines whether or not we should have access to certain roles and places (literally and figuratively). At this stage we may begin to pursue fulfillment of personal potential.[15]

Level 4. We are able to step back enough from the social environment to learn and generate an internal seat of judgment, or personal authority, that evaluates and makes choices about external expectations. We make meaning of our lives and selves by aligning with our own belief system, ideology, or personal code. We develop the ability to self-direct, take stands, set limits, and create and regulate our boundaries based on own voice. At this stage, we are developing our independence. However, we know that independence is not enough in an interconnected and interdependent world.

Level 5. We seek to further a cause beyond ourselves and to experience relationships beyond the boundaries of our own identities and ideas. We can step back from and reflect on the limits of our own ideology or personal authority. We see that any one approach, idea, system or self-organization is in some way partial or incomplete. We can be friendlier toward contradiction and opposites and seek to hold on to multiple perspectives. Our understanding of ourselves is through our ability not to confuse our internal consistency with completeness. We constantly reevaluate and learn rather than cling to comfort. We can cope with and reconcile inner and external conflicts. We can navigate volatility, uncertainty, complexity, and ambiguity (VUCA). This type of growth enhances the quality of life of living organisms, ecosystems, and societies and includes an increase in complexity, sophistication, and maturity.[16]

Ego development research has found that 80% of people are in level three and four, with only 7 to 17% of adults ever reaching level 5.[17] Kegan's research has shown more specifically that almost 60% of adults have not grown beyond level 3; the majority of us are stuck there.[18] The highest levels of psychological functioning allows us to have more sophisticated ways of perceiving ourselves and others. It requires three parts that need to be integrated: cognitive, emotional, and motivational. First, we need deep and broad insight into self, others, and the world. Second, we need complex emotion regulation especially in the face conflict and ambiguity. Finally, we need a motivational orientation that transcends self-interest and invests in the well-being of others and the world.

We have made declarations about our desire to dismantle racism and advance racial equity or racial justice. We sit around waiting, hoping, begging, craving, wishing for change to happen. Meanwhile, we maintain the exact same thinking, social circles, organizational structures, and habits we have always had. We say we want to change racial oppression, but we do not develop any new skills or approaches that will get us closer to that goal. Many of us do not even understand what we mean when we say we want racial equity or social justice. We can waste our time and energy hoping for things to change and judging people around us for not doing enough. Or we can concentrate on what is in our control and start taking action. **"You can't wring your hands and roll up your sleeves at the same time."** In other words, we can sit around worrying *or* we can take action, but we cannot do both. So we might as well roll up our sleeves and get to work. We can and must take responsibility for ourselves and each other. Let's not leave

> This quote is attributed to Patricia Schroeder, former U.S. House Representative for Colorado. However, I first learned it from the wonderful Dr. Robert Macy, trauma expert, during a conversation where he humble-bragged about some really famous and important person telling him that their grandfather used to say this, which I am not disputing…I know better.

progress to the whims of other people. If we want racial justice and freedom, we have to focus on what is in our control to take deliberate action. This is how we get closer to the world we say we want.

For example, it is not enough to say that we need to address the racial wealth gap. We have to spend time learning about it, why it exists, and then identify the most impactful levers of action that will shift the dynamics towards equity. Then we identify how we as people in our personal and professional lives will contribute to applying the weight of our actions to the levers that will be most effective. For some they do their personal shopping with businesses owned by BIPOC as much as possible. For others they ensure their organization is contracting with businesses owned by BIPOC. Some of us will ensure that we have hiring and promotional processes that ensure BIPOC and other understated groups earn incomes that match their contributions and are comparable to other employees.

Here is the really powerful thing about habits: Our identity emerges out of them. The process of being intentional about our individual and collective habits is the process of becoming ourselves. The social realities we have created because of racism is cyclical. Our daily social practices are stealthily guided by racism-infected social structures that we do not realize we are reproducing through our habits. In getting closer to ourselves, we can be closer with each other.

In the next Chapter, I discuss the human condition, development, and habits that our system of racism is built upon. Throughout this book, we will explore more about these habits and how we can choose for ourselves who we want to be and adjust our habits accordingly.

Chapter 1. The Habit of Racism

1.   Merriam-Webster.com Dictionary. Habit. Merriam-Webster. Accessed September 6, 2020, https://www.merriam-webster.com/dictionary/habit

2.   Duhigg C. *The Power of Habit: Why We Do What We Do in Life and Business.* 2014.

3.   Bonilla-Silva E. *Racism without Racists: Color-Blind Racism ad the Persistence of Racial Inequality in America.* Fourth ed. Rowman & Littlefiled Publishers, Inc.; 2014:363.

4.   Clear J. *Atomic Habits: An Easy & Proven Way to Build Good Habits & Break Bad Ones.* Avery an Imprint of Penguin Random House LLC; 2018.

5.   Allen TW. *The Invention of the White Race.* vol II: The Origin of Racial Oppression in Anglo-America. Verso; 2012.

6.   Maslow AH. A Theory of Human Motivation. *Psychological review.* 1943;50(4):370-396. doi:http://dx.doi.org.ezproxy.neu.edu/10.1037/h0054346

7.   Koltko-Rivera ME. Rediscovering the later version of Maslow's hierarchy of needs: Self-transcendence and opportunities for theory, research, and unification. *Review of General Psychology.* 2006;10(4):302-317. doi:10.1037/1089-2680.10.4.302

8.   Maslow AH. *Motivation and Personality.* Third ed. Longman, An imprint of Addison Wesley Longman, Inc.; 1987.

9.   Harter JK, Schmidt FL, Agrawal S, Plowman SK, Blue A. *The Relationship Between Engagement at Work and Organizational Outcomes: 2016 Q12® Meta-Analysis.* 2019. https://news.gallup.com/reports/257567/gallup-q12-meta-analysis-report.aspx

10.   Noltemeyer A, James AG, Bush K, Bergen D, Barrios V, Patton J. The Relationship between Deficiency Needs and Growth Needs: The Continuing Investigation of Maslow's Theory. *Child & Youth Services.* 2020:1-19. doi:10.1080/0145935X.2020.1818558

11.   Snarey J, Kohlberg L, Noam G. Ego development in perspective: Structural stage, functional phase, and cultural age-period models. *Developmental Review.* 1983;3(3):303-338. doi:10.1016/0273-2297(83)90018-7

12.   Hardiman R, Wijeyesinghe CL, Jackson BW. *New perspectives on racial identity development: A theoretical and practical anthology.* 2001:129.

13.   Helms JE. *Black and White racial identity: Theory, research and practices.* vol null. null. 1990:null.

14.   Loevinger J. *Paradigms of Personality.* W H Freeman & Co; 1987.

15.   Manners J, Durkin K. A critical review of the validity of ego development theory and its measurement. *Journal of Personality Assessment.* Dec 2001;77(3):541-67. doi:10.1207/S15327752JPA7703_12

16.   Capra F, Luisi PL. *The Systems View of Life: A Unifying Vision.* Cambridge University Press; 2014.

17.   Daniels D, Saracino T, Fraley M, Christian J, Pardo S. Advancing Ego Development in Adulthood Through Study of the Enneagram System of Personality. *Jouirnal of Adult Development.* 2018;25(4):229-241. doi:10.1007/s10804-018-9289-x

18.   Kegan R, Laskow Lahey L. *An Everyone Culture: Becoming a Deliberately Developmental Organization.* Harvard Business Review Press; 2016.

2. THERE ARE LAYERS & NUANCE TO THIS

"Racism is a historically rooted system of dehumanizing ideologies that reinforce the concept of whiteness: the superiority and power of white people and the inferiority and powerlessness of people of color. The ideology of whiteness results in conscious and unconscious internalized, interpersonal, and institutional habits that harm both People of Color and White People in different ways." -All Aces, Inc.

The system of racism has multiple components that operate in harmony to create and propel it. We become cogs in the system through our conditioned, habitual support. This concept is captured by the definition of a system:[1]

- ➲ An organized society or social situation regarded as stultifying or oppressive
- ➲ A regularly interacting or interdependent group of items forming a unified whole
- ➲ A group of interacting bodies under the influence of related forces
- ➲ An organized set of doctrines, ideas, or principles usually intended to explain the arrangement or working of a systematic whole.

This definition provides context on why the four interrelated layers of racism is a system: ideological, internalized, interpersonal, and institutional. Think of these layers as a Venn diagram with each circle contributing to the other (See Figure 1 on the next page). At the center is ideology, which represents its foundational role in all the other layers.

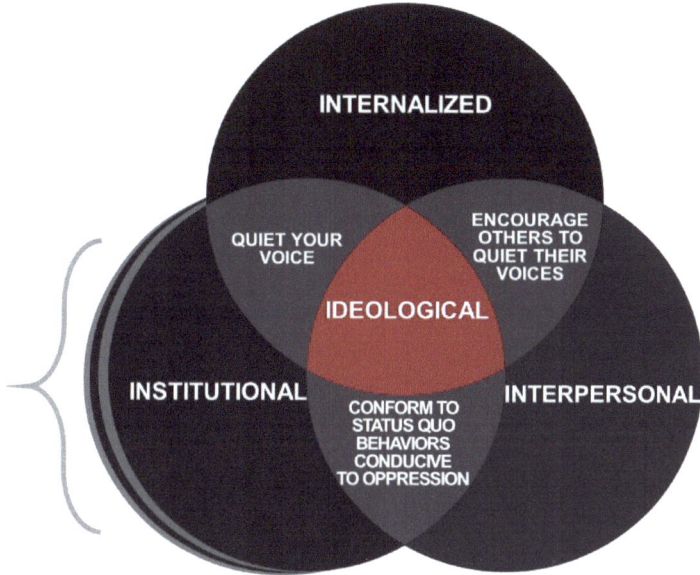

Figure 4: Layers of Systemic Racism

Here is where even more complexity comes in: Racism does not exist in isolation. It has been built on top of a foundation of the human condition: our default tendencies that exist because of the way our brain is wired (neuroscience); how we receive cues about ideas and expectations from people and organizations we encounter (sociology); and how we think about the world, ourselves, and others (psychology). It is this complicated set of interconnected interactions that drives our behavior. While not a neuroscientist, sociologist, or psychologist, I am a nerd and perpetual learner. In writing this book, I had several moments of clarity inspired by concepts from these fields of study as well as others such as engineering, biology, and philosophy.

These non-racism-related sources have furtherer clarified for me the thinking and behaviors that are harmful to our human development. Much of the thinking that continues to uphold the system of racism is aligned with thinking that is harmful to our personal and professional development. Even when we are engaged with racism workshops, there are messages we receive that reinforce ideas that are not helpful.

In many workshops, people are told that "People of Color cannot be racist because they do not have any power" or "White People need to do the work." I know what is meant to be conveyed by these statements: the system of racism was created by and benefits White People at the expense and invisibility of People of Color. However, it subliminally reinforces the oppressive narrative of powerlessness for People of Color. Furthermore, the concept of who is a "racist" is unproductive in a society where we all have pockets of incompetence about racism and are at times part of the problem and the solution (White People and People of Color). It allows all of us to hide behind the finger pointed at someone else instead of putting energy into learning, critical reflection, conscious thinking, and intentional behavior for ourselves and our organizations.

Just as there are layers (most people refer to them as levels) of racism that overlap and interact with one another, there are layers of power. And each of us, including Black, Indigenous, and People of Color (BIPOC), has access to these layers of power. This is difficult to untangle because we do not often discuss what power is and how it works. The most helpful framework on power for me has been from sociology:[2]

- ➲ **Power Within**: This is our sense of self-worth and self-knowledge. This includes an ability to recognize our own uniqueness and contributions while respecting other people's. 'Power within' is the capacity to create a vision for our own lives and have hope in our own possibilities.
- ➲ **Power To**: This is our ability to take action. This type of power builds upon 'power within' to create new possibilities for agency in our own lives, communities, and organizations. As we build power within and power to, we uncover and unleash what has been invisible power – action and possibilities we did not even know were available to us (see Chapter 4: Internalized for more on invisible power).
- ➲ **Power With**: This is our collective strength. It exponentially expands the amount and impact of individual talents and knowledge by weaving us together for collective action, mutual support, and solidarity. It can help build bridges within and across different races and ethnicities to act on shared struggles.
- ➲ **Power Over**: This is about controlling power, which involves taking it from someone else, and then, using it to dominate and prevent others from gaining any. This is how we normally think about power, as a limited commodity (more on this in Chapter 6: Institutional).

In addition to warping our sense of power, racism and other forms of oppression produce a lot of waste: (1) misdirected energy in reinforcing conformity that upholds the system of racism which significantly limits innovation;[3] (2) talent that is overlooked because of dehumanizing thinking and a lack of historical context;[4] (3) loss of actual money in the American GDP;[5] and (4) missed opportunities to collaborate across businesses, nonprofits, government, and community members on the complex, interdependent problems of our time.[6]

Challenges and Opportunities of Our Humanity

The qualities we need on the journey towards advancing racial equity are the same ones we need to grow and learn as human beings: humility, hope, and hard work.

Many of us have been exposed to Sigmund Freud's id, ego, and superego framing of the psyche (the totality of the human mind, consciousness, and unconsciousness). The id is the animalistic part of the unconscious mind where our instinctual behavior for survival (eating, sleep, etc.) live. The ego is considered the conscious mind; and superego is our critical inner voice (we will come back to this in the next chapter). The ego mediates between the id, superego, and reality. It is also responsible for our sense of personal identity. Ego strength is the ability of the ego to deal effectively with the demands of the id, the superego, and reality.[7] It helps us to differentiate between representations of what is external—of the object world—from representations of what is internal—of the self or of mental life. Dr. Eric Berne further broke the ego down into three ego states: the parent (control and rules), adult (thoughtful and respectful of their own and others dignity), and child (emotionally driven, either follows directions or rebels against authority, not respectful of other people's dignity). The ability of our ego to make sense of and engage with the world depends on our skill level in showing up as our best selves (adult ego state).

The controversial B.F. Skinner took a position on human behavior that seems to disregard the id, ego, and superego. Skinner believed that examining the unconscious or hidden motives of human beings was a waste of time, because the only thing worth researching was outward behaviors.[8] Skinner defines human behavior not as a set of *actions* motivated by us, but a set of *responses* that have been consistently reinforced through conditioning by the environment in which we live. To improve the lives of people in our society, he believed that we have to change which behaviors are being reinforced, both directly and indirectly, through the choices our culture allows or provides. Skinner claimed that continuing to uphold the idea of "autonomous man," is detrimental to ourselves and the improvement of our society. He tended to focus on the role of consequences in choice architecture (the way we structure choices available to people so we can influence them to make *better* choices). Some of us are familiar with choice architecture through Cass Sunstein's book, *Nudge*. Nudging focuses on the role of what comes before our behavior when analyzing choice architecture.[9] In both instances, the foundations are built on the power of forces outside ourselves that drive our behavior.

As with many things, the truth seems to lie at an intersection. We have a rich inner world that most of us have not learned about or learned how to navigate *and* our external environment influences our inner world *AND* our inner world can influence our environment. The less insight we have into ourselves, the more our external environment can manipulate us. The stronger our sense of self, the less influenced we are and the more influential we can be.

There are a set of key characteristics of a weak ego versus a strong ego.[10] Another way to organize the ego-strength concept is by examining each element of ego functioning.[11] The traits for a weak ego or underdeveloped ego functioning eerily align with many of the characteristics that are associated with what has been termed white supremacy culture or what I have been referring to as whiteness (See Chapter 3 for more on whiteness). It also closely aligns with human irrationality and the opposite of what we need to be resilient. The following paragraphs provide considerations for healthy ego functioning and protective factors that can build, sustain, or challenge our resilience.

Self-Awareness. The first step to self-awareness and good mental health is understanding our defenses, motives, and conflicts. The most basic function of the self-consciousness system is awareness of the processes that are influencing us. When we have high levels of insight, we know how we feel, what makes us tick, when and why we have conflicts, and what we need to feel fulfilled. In the social theory of power, this is referred to as "power within." When we have poor insight, we engage in more primitive psychological defenses like denial, and are clueless about who we are or try to convince ourselves we are something we are not. The more insight we have, the more quickly we can make sense of ourselves in difficult situations. Our ego manages all the defense mechanisms that are listed below. This ego function can help us maintain stability and improve our condition when we are depressed.[12] Racism is a major barrier to understanding ourselves and why we do what we do. This part of ego functioning is directly related to all layers of racism (ideological, internalized, interpersonal, and institutional).

Agency + Self-Direction. When we have agency (what the social theory of power refers to as "power to"), we see ourselves as able to control key aspects of our environment and guide our behavior with purpose. We can engage in self-directed behavior, effectively guiding our actions toward goals across time, can manage impulses, and are resilient in the face of setbacks. In contrast, when we do not have agency, we have an external locus of control, experience life as happening to us, have no direction, and often feel dependent on the whims of fate or the environment in terms of what happens to us. We also are impulsive, responding to the needs of the moment rather than inhibiting our immediate desires for longer-term goals.

Self-Esteem. Closely related to agency is esteem, the extent to which we respect and value ourselves. Feeling good about ourselves, being able to accept our faults or limitations, and having basic compassionate feelings toward ourselves is extremely important. In contrast to self-discipline, although many with low self-esteem have poor self-directedness, it is possible that we might have high self-directness but may also be extremely self-critical, and lacking in acceptance and compassion, which is why the two are conceptually separated. Recent research has emphasized self-compassion as a better way of fostering mental health than trying to directly raise self-esteem. In confronting racism, we have to be able to separate the mistake from our identity and self-esteem. However, we cannot gain self-compassion by justifying our thinking and behavior. Mistakes are a normal part of learning. You can be a good person who caused harm to another person or yourself. However, it does not have to define us unless we keep mindlessly justifying the impact.[13] True self compassion is a process. Failure is a badge of effort and a source of learning and growth: Making mistakes and correcting them build the bridges to advanced learning.[14, 15] To fail is a deeply human experience. Each of us, no matter our background, skillset, or life story, will fail spectacularly at least once. However, the fact that it is a shared, common experience does not mean that it is easy or fun. Furthermore, in a winner-takes-all, scarcity culture that prioritizes success at all costs, it means that many will look down on us when the inevitable happens: How will we see ourselves? Learning to be okay with making mistakes, big or small, is a critical skill—one tied not only to resilience but also, perhaps, to future success. Some research has found that young scientists who experienced a significant setback early in their career actually went on to greater success than scientists who had seen early wins.[16]

Relationship Management. A healthy ego makes it possible for us to have mutually satisfying relationships. This requires the ability to see ourselves and others as three dimensional. Our "selves" exist within interdependent networks of other people. We initially understand ourselves through the lens of mirrored others, and our identity is very much about narrating and legitimizing our actions to others. Therefore, our sense of self emerges in close relationship to our sense of others (and how they treat us). While insight refers to the capacity to understand ourselves, empathy refers to the capacity to understand others. This empathy is a precursor to our ability to have social awareness and relationship management skills which both make up the social competence of emotional intelligence.

Inner Narrative. Our inner narrative is based on the degree of integration across identities, having clear purpose, and thematic coherence. We all alternate between two parts of ourselves: (1) self-states and (2) various social groups we belong to and roles that we fill. The issue is to what extent does the ego have a meta-narrative that coherently connects the different parts. Many of us lack a basic storyline that makes our lives meaningful. Without it, we behave in inconsistent ways. As a result, we can feel a vague sense of conflict. We cannot quite put our finger on what is wrong because we do not have an overarching narrative that brings our lives into context.

Worldview. To develop a more complicated, purposeful, coherent narrative, we must place that in the context of a worldview. To gauge our ego functioning, we must determine how developed our philosophical point of view is: The degree of sophistication of that perspective, its complexity and breadth, and the extent to which it provides us with a sense of direction toward what is real. Our worldview is a foundational part of ego functioning. This is one of the many reasons it is important to understand how internalized whiteness plays out in our perspectives and lives…ideological racism is a filter that distorts our worldview and disrupts a healthy inner narrative.

External Realities. This is not considered a component of ego functioning. However, our external realities—our families, communities, organizations/institutions, and larger society—are important considerations because they are oftentimes not in our direct control. They can be potential protective factors for, harmful to, or influenceable by our resilience. Some of the criticism of resilience is that many people frame it as solely an individual trait and, as such, ignore the larger social context. However, these social dimensions of personal resilience have decades of research that incorporate a more accurate depiction of our complex interdependency with other people and larger society.[17] The Bioecological Model of Human Development by Urie Bronfenbrenner is an example of a way of mapping out complicated, interrelated components of influences on our lives.

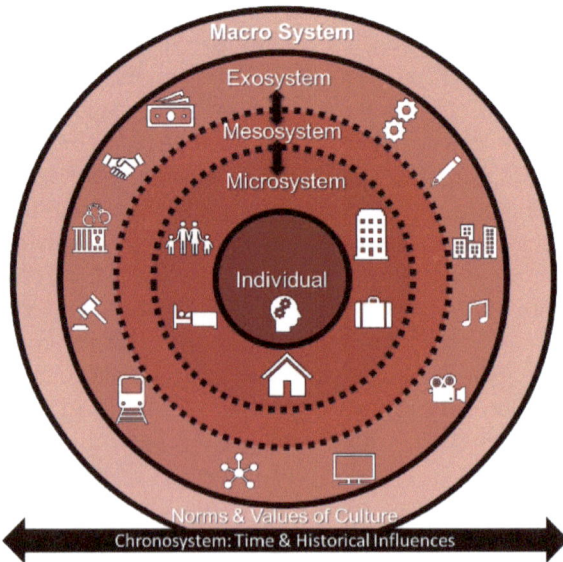

Figure 5: Urie Bronfenbrenner's Bioecological Model of Human Development

On the other hand, we are not just influenced, **we have the power to**

influence. Although we do not have direct control of other people and organizations, we can affect their development and behavior through the intentional development of our own knowledge and skills that support our resilience. Letting go of blame and shame creates the space we need to focus our energy on our own responsibilities in confronting racism and advancing racial equity. If I think it is someone else's work to do, then I have to wait for them to get it done and I will likely be waiting forever. But if I own my responsibility, then I put the power back into my own hands to take action.

Here, we can see the bystander effect at work in this dynamic. The bystander effect demonstrates that the likelihood we will receive help decreases when others are present, and it further decreases if you are BIPOC. In other words, we are less likely to act if other people are around, and even less likely when other people are present *and* the people suffering are BIPOC. We have been acting as collective bystanders with no sense of shared responsibility for confronting racism and advancing racial equity.[18]

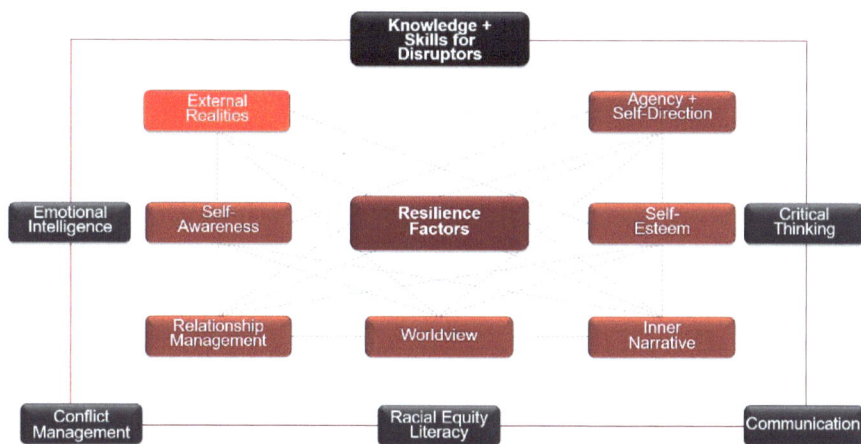

Figure 6: Resilience Factors with Knowledge + Skills for Disruptors

Some of the ways we sabotage our own resilience – which limits our ability to manage ourselves and influence situations – are unproductive defense mechanisms. The following is a synthesized list of defense mechanisms to understand ways we deal with situations that are uncomfortable as well as several that are more constructive approaches.[19]

Denial: When we use denial, we simply refuse to accept a reality. In the same ways that people deny racism exists beyond someone hating another person or the fact that each of us has played a role as a passive conductor of oppression.

Regression: Regression means mentally going back to an earlier stage of development (see Chapter 1). In severe cases, we can become so removed from our current stage of development that we cannot function normally. Milder regression often involves small comfort-seeking behaviors. In the context of racism, it is easy to get stuck at lower stages of development that are driven by our desire to be accepted or to remain comfortable.

Intellectualization + Dissociation + Compartmentalization: This category is about the ways we use thinking to avoid our feelings and ourselves. When we intellectualize, we use thinking to avoid feeling. We shut down all of our emotions and try to approach a situation solely from a rational standpoint, especially when the expression of emotions would be appropriate. Dissociation is when we separate from our thoughts, feelings, and even our sense of identity. During and right after a traumatic event, we may have a surreal feeling, as if we are watching the event on a streaming service rather than living it. Mild dissociation can help us get through extremely difficult situations. Compartmentalization is a lesser form of dissociation, where parts of us are separated from awareness of other parts and behaving as if one had separate sets of values. BIPOC may try to disassociate from our painful experiences with racism. White People may try to compartmentalize internalized societal norms and values from their conscious beliefs in racial equity and social justice. We all tend to intellectualize in moments when expressing our emotions is most appropriate.

Displacement: We use displacement as a mechanism when we change the target of our impulse. We may have an impulse to behave violently towards White People because of injustices, but it is not emotionally or physically safe, so instead, we turn our violence on other People of Color. Similarly, we see White People who understand racism may really be angry with themselves but take it out on other White People who are still learning. This is also related to projection (if they cannot see racism operating within themselves).

Reaction Formation: Reaction formation means doing the opposite of our unwanted or negative emotions. When we feel that our impulses are unacceptable, we do the opposite, trying to convince ourselves and/or others that we do not have those feelings. It is a way of trying to prove that we are worthy when we have impulses that we think are wrong. We are incapable or unwilling to express the negative emotions, and instead publicly express overly positive sentiments to demonstrate our lack of negative emotions.

Projection: When we use projection, we see our own traits in other people while not seeing them in ourselves. By focusing on the other person, we distract ourselves from seeing the trait within us. Through projection, we try to protect our ego by shifting the problem. This is relevant to both White People and People of Color. It is easy to other people's contributions to racism, but not our own.

Rationalization: Rationalization is justifying our thoughts and behavior by putting them into a different light or offering a different explanation for the perceptions or behaviors in the face of a changing reality. Nearly each of us has rationalized our behavior at one time or another. Rationalization means making excuses. We may do something we feel is unacceptable, but we do not want to be seen as a person who would do that without reason. We try to use logic to explain our choice. Unfortunately, the logic is flawed.

Sublimation: A more productive defense mechanism is sublimation. When we have an unwanted impulse, thought, or emotion, we may channel it into a more acceptable behavior. When we experience undesired impulse, we can redirect that energy into something more productive. When we feel discomfort from the cognitive dissonance of realizing our behavior contributed or is contributing to racism, we can turn the discomfort into curiosity to learn how we can be better and do better as disruptors of oppression. A type of sublimation is altruism. We may become very altruistic after we experience a great pain. Instead of falling into depression, we put our energy into helping others. Another related defense is humor. We may use humor to help us deal with painful or uncomfortable situations. If something happens that we cannot change, laughing about it can help us get through it.

Compensation. The second more productive defense is to psychologically counterbalance perceived weaknesses by emphasizing strength in other arenas. By emphasizing one's strengths, a person recognizes they cannot be strong at all things and in all areas in their lives. When done measuredly, compensation helps us reinforce our self-esteem and self-image.

Assertiveness. Assertiveness is the emphasis of our needs or thoughts in a manner that is respectful, direct and firm. Communication styles exist on a continuum, ranging from passive to aggressive, with assertiveness falling in the middle. People who communicate in a passive manner tend to be good listeners, but rarely speak up for themselves or their own needs in a relationship. People who communicate in an aggressive manner tend to end up in leadership positions, but often lack the ability to listen with empathy to others and their ideas and needs. When we are assertive, we speak up for ourselves, express our opinions or needs in a respectful yet firm manner, and listen when we are being spoken to. In order to be disruptors of oppression, we need to build our communication skills so we can advocate for more just treatment and decisions.

As we build our knowledge and skills to disrupt racism and other forms of oppression, we begin to find our own voice. As we find our own voice and hold on to it, we can help other people find and keep their voice. I refer to this process as the Developmental Approach to Resilience and Racial Equity (DARRE). Each of the Knowledge + Skills for Disruptors are embedded throughout the DARRE model on the next page.

In the following chapters, resilience factors and the knowledge and skills

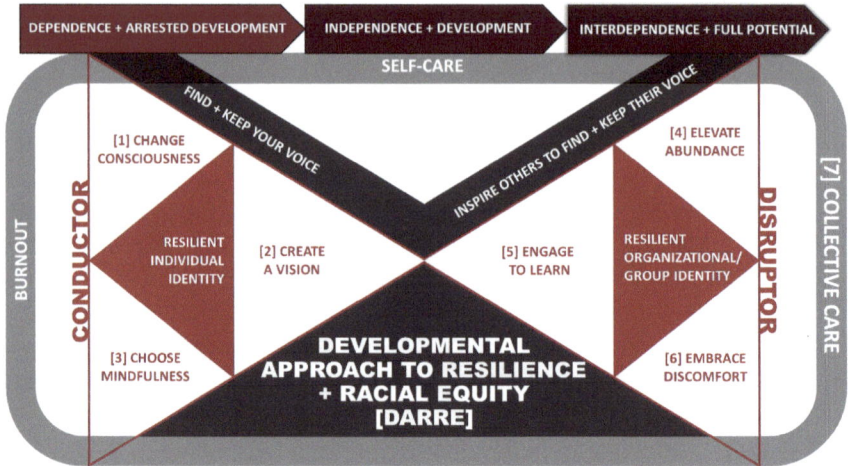

Figure 7: Developmental Approach to Resilience + Racial Equity

for disruptors will be summarized based on their relationship with each layer of racism and racial equity: ideological, internalized, interpersonal, and institutional. Within each layer, we will explore what they mean to us, how they work, and the related habits. The final chapter, Disruptors of Oppression, brings everything together to summarize the content and create a clear pathway for people and organizations to shift from habits that support the system of racism to those that support the system of racial equity…habits that support collective freedom.

Chapter 2. There are Layers and Nuance to This

1.   Merriam-Webster. System. Merriam-Webster.com dictionary. Accessed 12/23/2019, https://www.merriam-webster.com/dictionary/system

2.   Rowlands J. *Questioning Empowerment: Working with Women in Honduras.* Oxfam; 1997.

3.   Trenerry B, Paradies Y. Organizational Assessment: An Overlooked Approach to Managing Diversity and Addressing racism in the Workplace. *Journal of Diversity Management.* 2012;7(1):11-26.

4.   Brief AP, Dietz J, Cohen RR, Pugh SD, Vaslow JB. Just Doing Business: Modern Racism and Obedience to Authority as Explanations for Employment Discrimination. *Organizational Behavior and Human Decision Processes.* 2000/01/01/ 2000;81(1):72-97. doi:https://doi.org/10.1006/obhd.1999.2867

5.   Akala A. Cost of Racism: U.S. Economy Lost $16 Trillion Because of Discrimination, Bank Says. NPR. Accessed 9/25/2020, 2020. https://www.npr.org/sections/live-updates-protests-for-racial-justice/2020/09/23/916022472/cost-of-racism-u-s-economy-lost-16-trillion-because-of-discrimination-bank-says?utm_source=twitter.com&utm_term=nprnews&utm_medium=social&utm_campaign=npr

6.   Glasberg SD, Shannon D. *Political Sociology: Oppression, Resistance, and the State.* Pine Forge, an Imprint of Sage Publications; 2011.

7.   Besharat MA, Ramesh S, Moghimi E. Spiritual health mediates the relationship between ego-strength and adjustment to heart disease. *Health Psychology Open.* Jan-Jun 2018;5(1):1-8. doi:10.1177/2055102918782176

8.   Skinner BF. *Beyond Freedom & Dignity.* Hackett Publishing Company, Inc.; 1971.

9.   Thaler RH, Sunstein C. *Nudge: Improving Decisions About Health, Wealth, and Happiness.* Penguin Books Ltd.; 2009.

10.   The Editors of Encyclopaedia Britannica. Ego. Encyclopædia Britannica, Inc. Updated November 16, 2018. Accessed September 06, 2020, 2020.

11.   Henriques G. The Elements of Ego Functioning. Accessed 9/7/2020, 2020. https://www.psychologytoday.com/us/blog/theory-knowledge/201306/the-elements-ego-functioning

12.   Beck AT. *Cognitive Therapy and the Emotional Disorders: A Major Exploration of an Influential Approach to the Understanding and Treatment of Mental Illness.* International Unversities Press; 1979.

13.   Tavris C, Aronson E. *Mistakes Were Made (But Not by Me): Why We Justify Foolish Beliefs, Bad Decisions and Hurtful Acts.* Houghton Mifflin Harcourt Publishing Company; 2015.

14.   Brown PC, Roediger HL, McDaniel MA. *Make It Stick: The Science of*

Successful Learning. The Belknap Press of Harvard University Press; 2014.

15.   Paul R, Elder L. *Critical Thinking: Tools for Taking Charge of Your Professional and Personal Life.* Second ed. Pearson Education, Inc.; 2014.

16.   Allen S. Early Career Failures Can Make You Stronger in the Long Run. Kellogg School of Management at Northwestern University. Accessed 11/8/2020, https://insight.kellogg.northwestern.edu/article/early-setbacks-failure-career-success

17.   Fleming J, Ledogar RJ. Resilience, an Evolving Concept: A Review of Literature Relevant to Aboriginal Research. *Pimatisiwin/PMC Canada Author Manuscripts.* 2008;6(2):7-23.

18.   Murrell AJ. Why someone did not stop them? Aversive racism and the responsibility of bystanders. *Equality, Diversity and Inclusion: An International Journal.* 2020;ahead-of-print(ahead-of-print)doi:10.1108/edi-07-2020-0191

19.   Grohol JM. 15 Common Defense Mechanisms. Psych Central. Accessed 11/11/2020, https://psychcentral.com/lib/15-common-defense-mechanisms/

3. IDEOLOGICAL: CULTIVATING THE CRAVING

"You have to decide who you are and force the world to deal with you, not with its idea of you." – James Baldwin

There are many ideas that serve as the default settings programmed into us based on how we are wired (neuroscience), how we are conditioned by people and organizations around us (sociology), and how those things influence the way we think (psychology) and therefore behave. These ideas establish the framing we use to understand and navigate ourselves, each other, and our organizations.

Default settings are usually associated with technology. When we get a device, like a cell phone, it comes preprogrammed with settings or options that determine everything from the ringtone to which alert notifications we receive. Specific options, whether helpful or not, are available to us (and others) because we have not customized them for ourselves.

Ideological racism – and the whiteness and anti-blackness that comes with it – are our default settings. Ideological racism is the cultivation of ideas that reinforce the inferiority and powerlessness of People of Color and the superiority and power of White People, while dehumanizing both groups in the process. Whiteness, as previously described, is the subliminal craving that ideological racism cultivates in all of us with detrimental—albeit different—impacts for White People and People of Color.

From infancy, the foundational ideas of racism are omnipresent. We are bombarded with messages, behaviors, and symbols that subtly preprogram default settings into us. This programming frames how we make sense of the world, including each other as individuals and as members of social groups, in this case, race. Ideological racism has a major impact on our mental health through the way it molds our worldview—which is a major component of healthy ego functioning and resilience factors. Our worldview influences how we make sense of the world, others, and ourselves. If we want to have a coherent narrative for ourselves (inner narrative), we have to establish a coherent and sophisticated narrative of the world around us that respects its volatility. Our effort to avoid making ourselves more comfortable and oversimplifying facilitates our ability to have a consistent orientation toward reality.

Dealing with internalized whiteness, defining an antiracist, racially equitable lifestyle, and becoming comfortable with communicating about racism have been identified as key challenges that White People experience.[1] These are also challenges that Black, Indigenous, and People of Color (BIPOC) face. These shared challenges are among the many reasons why I frame racism as a problem that is harmful to all of us that requires collective action. What further complicates our challenges with racism is that we are conditioned to have certain non-racism-specific beliefs that set us up to believe ideas that facilitate racism. Furthermore, we are socialized to avoid reflecting on the ways we are socialized.[2]

American Ideas that Pave the Road to Racism

Another way to look at how society's flawed ideas lay the groundwork for ideological racism and oppression is from Stephen Covey's *7 Habits of Highly Effective People*. He lists some of the "most common human challenges"[3] and I have summarized and remixed them in the following paragraphs.

Fear and Insecurity. Many of us are gripped with fear. We fear for the future. We feel vulnerable in the workplace and are afraid of losing our jobs that allow us to provide for our families. This deficit-based thinking often fosters a resignation to riskless living and to co-dependency with others. Our culture's common response to this problem is to become more and more independent which, although important, ignores that we live in an interdependent reality requiring skills that are far beyond independence.

Impatience + Urgency. People want everything now. Our society colludes by continuing to make it easy for us to get what we want when we want it. This includes everything from results to reports to societal change. However, we need to balance the need to meet today's demands with the need to invest in the capabilities and action that will produce tomorrow's success. We can invest in developing and implementing our capabilities for resilience, racial equity, and social justice and allow those skills to shift how we live our lives and operate our organizations. There is no need to create a false dichotomy or a competing set of false choices between urgency and capabilities building. However, this is *not* an excuse for organizations to avoid taking immediate action on the issues we can when BIPOC bring them to our attention.

Blame and Victimism. Wherever there is a problem, there is usually finger-pointing. Society is addicted to playing the victim. If only this person/group weren't that way then I could [fill in the blank]. Blaming provides temporary relief of the pain, but it also chains us to the problems we are complaining about. We are likely to take no action because we see the problem as someone else's fault. We absolve ourselves from taking the actions that we can within our circles of influence. This applies to BIPOC and White People. For BIPOC, this is not about victim-blaming, but taking our power to be change agents in our own liberation. No one can give us freedom. We have to lead the way.

Hopelessness. The children of blame are cynicism and hopelessness. When we succumb to believing that we are only victims of our circumstances and give in to helplessness, we lose hope, we lose drive, and we settle into resignation. We become passengers on the road of life, which ironically, breeds more situations where we are helpless victims and therefore more hopelessness. This is why it is so key to take intentional action in our circle of influence. Building our resilience to racism is not about surviving it, but disrupting and dismantling it within ourselves, how we engage with others, and how we structure and run our organizations.

Busyness. Life in our society is focused on doing a lot of things, many of which do not matter in the larger scheme of things. Balance and peace of mind are not produced by busyness. They are products of when we have a clear sense of our highest priorities and values and live with focus and integrity towards maintaining and evaluating them. We see busyness in a number of people's responses to feedback that their actions have caused harm to BIPOC. The response is often a word salad that the individual or organization serve up to absolve them from the harm they have caused. For example: Some of my closest friends are [fill in the blank BIPOC race or ethnicity]. I donate money to [fill in the blank organization]. Our company hired a DEI position and host events celebrating diversity all the time. The busyness of random activities that are not part of a clear strategy, commitment to action, metrics to evaluate, and accountability to BIPOC and the larger community keeps us on the hamster wheel of oppression.

What's In it for Me? Our culture teaches us that we need to be rugged individuals...pull ourselves up by our bootstraps. It says that we are in constant competition...with everyone. The veil of racism and other forms of oppression tend to focus our competitiveness on underestimated and marginalized people in our society (BIPOC, immigrants, etc.). Although many of us can put on the appearance of being happy for others, our inner world is on fire with jealousy of the individual achievements of other people, especially if they do not look like us. However, true greatness in this interdependent world is for those who achieve through an abundance mindset that strives to work selflessly with mutual respect for mutual benefit.

The Hunger to Be Understood. There are few needs of the human heart greater than the need to be understood: To have a voice that is heard, respected, and valued. For many of us, that translates into influence and the best way to influence others is through communication. However, we think communicating is a one-way street where we wait our turn to say what we want because we are just trying to listen to respond. The reality is that real influence is governed by mutual understanding which requires us to deeply listen. In discussions about racism, this is particularly difficult if we see ourselves as the victim and others as the villain…then no one is a human being with agency in the situation.

Conflict and Differences. Our common humanity is powerful, and in the same breath, we are also very different. Sometimes we have competing values, motivations, and objectives. Naturally, conflicts arise because of these differences. Because of our competitive societal worldview, conflict and differences are about winning as much as we can. The challenges of our times require us to problem solve through conflict and find co-created, thoughtful approaches that can address various needs (which means we all have to give a little). It also means that there are no easy answers; we have to work through the problems together. Conflict is a clarifier. Building and using conflict management skills supports our ability to have deeper relationships with ourselves and people we encounter. These skills help us work through our respective discomfort and self-centeredness to mutually reinforcing relationships.

Personal Stagnation. Conformity, consumption, and lack of self-awareness keep us locked into the boxes and limitations society has place on us. We will be in a total state of idiocracy (watch the movie) and dysfunction if we continue to go along with the crowd (which ever ones you belong to); consume products and entertainment more than we learn and create; and remain a stranger to ourselves and therefore others.

I have had to personally navigate unlearning many of these ways of thinking about the world. I am still excavating the harmful and unproductive concepts and framing of life and the world that show up in the most unexpected ways. I mentioned being angry at White People in the introduction for not understanding the hardships that racism places on BIPOC. Once I began to do more studying and listening, I understood where the ignorance manifests…the same place mine did: We were taught to be this way. I was taught that I was a helpless victim, and it just was not fair that I was always being mistreated, misunderstood, and disregarded. It locked me into a place of powerlessness. As I began to learn and grow, I began to see the hypocrisy of the ideas that fuel racism. I also began to see my own hypocrisy of thought. As with most things that matter in life, this is not an easy process. I have learned so much about myself and people around me. I continue to learn so I can avoid personal stagnation, which can open me back up to unhealthy habits of ideological racism.

The Habits of Ideological Racism

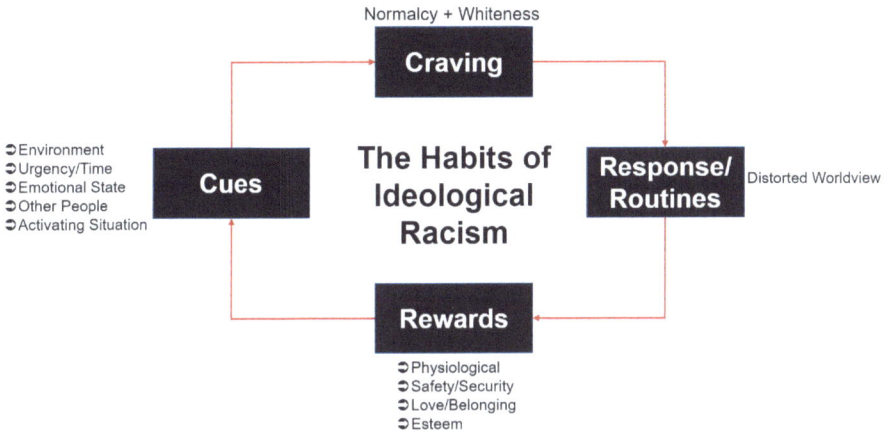

Normalcy + Whiteness

Craving

➲Environment
➲Urgency/Time
➲Emotional State
➲Other People
➲Activating Situation

Cues

The Habits of Ideological Racism

Response/ Routines

Distorted Worldview

Rewards

➲Physiological
➲Safety/Security
➲Love/Belonging
➲Esteem

Figure 8: The Habits of Ideological Racism

The habits of ideological racism produce a distorted worldview that locks us into unrealistic, neat little boxes that make us feel better. When accepted at face value, these patterns of ideas make our individual and collective power invisible. How we think about and treat culture is a good example.

The ways that we discuss culture are problematic because of the underlying assumptions in our discussions. First, there is an assumption that only Black, Indigenous, and People of Color (BIPOC) have culture, not White People. Second, there is an assumption that there is one monolithic or homogenous culture within a racial or ethnic group that can be learned in a training. Third, we pretend that American culture by default does not center the concepts of whiteness and antiblackness.

Even when we are teaching people about culture in relatively progressive contexts, we still use language that assumes BIPOC are culturally homogenous. "There are many other types of communities, however, that are not culturally homogenous, that are bonded in ways that have little bearing on culture."[4] This quote was meant to make a distinction between culture and community. However, they used BIPOC as the example of cultural homogeneity. This subtly reinforces the idea that we have culture to be sampled and experienced while White People just exist as the default and are regular – culture becomes synonymous with difference or diversity. Cultural difference is conveniently used to exclude or privilege certain groups of people. For Black People, parts of our cultures have been melded with historically used stereotypes of blackness to create a bastardized version that has infected us and the world around us. It has been weaponized as a tool of oppression to anyone deemed "the other." The strategies and tactics of racial oppression in America have been honed through their application on Indigenous People and African Americans. The xenophobic experiences of historical and present-day non-elite, non-White immigrants are an extension of these race-based strategies and tactics. Because the idea of White has changed over time, this includes all those who were not deemed White until the elite White People said so.[5, 6]

Researchers have found that the more time individuals spent watching network news, the more they endorsed stereotypes about Black Americans, including beliefs that Black People are intimidating, hostile, and violent or beliefs consistent with modern racism, such as the idea that "Blacks push themselves where they are not wanted."[7]

The other side of the spectrum is whiteness. Everyone is being compared against whiteness as the prototype for all human beings. Although most of the ideas about what we should expect from White People can be considered positive, that prototype is just as restrictive to White human development as stereotypes are for BIPOC's human development.

Ideological racism communicates to White People that they should buy-in to whiteness because as a White Person, you are the epitome of normalcy and all others are measured and valued against you. Without realizing it, to be American, human, or normal unconsciously translates into whiteness. By buying into whiteness, you as a White Person can feel comfortable seeing People of Color as only being a member of their racial group. However, *you* get to be an individual that is allowed (in James Baldwin's words) "to be released from the masses" of other White People.

The sheer volume of explicit and implicit information, visuals, and conversations that reinforce these racism-fueling ideas is no match for your good intentions as a White Person or as a Black, Indigenous, or People of Color trying to *save* BIPOC. Without ever saying it or realizing it, what we are trying to do in the process of saving BIPOC is communicating that you have some inherent greatness that makes you better than them and they just need to be more like prototypical White People. We are trying to fix their alleged moral bankruptcy with the illusory bounty that whiteness can offer.

If you are a Person of Color, the benefits of accepting whiteness means that you can become a gatekeeper. You have become an exception to the rules and all those *other* People of Color are defective. This is why you are going to facilitate who gets access to what, so no one messes it up for White People or the rest of us BIPOC who are exceptional.

Self-interest is a powerful psychological and social motivator in consciously and unconsciously being conductors of racism as BIPOC. This happens within racial and ethnic groups as well as across groups of People of Color. Rugged individualism (obsessive focus on individual efforts and benefits) encourages us to chase what we consider to be beneficial for ourselves without consideration for the wants, needs, or impacts to others, including those who share the same racial and ethnic identities.

Blackness + Whiteness + Identify

There are two concepts that undergird the ways we artificially organize the racial social hierarchy: Blackness and Whiteness. These concepts are rooted in stereotypical and protypical ideas of who Black People and White People are supposed to be. They both represent the end points on a spectrum of how we have organized America.

Although this book focuses on America, Black People are the international symbol of *the other*. The image of Black People has been distorted into a set of ideas that make our humanity invisible and shapes our experiences. Stereotypes are the ideas that create a pattern of thinking that leads to a devastating set of individual and collective behaviors.

I want to take the time to recognize that Indigenous People are the international symbol of *erasure*. They experience racial oppression through a denial of their right to exist on or control their own land and development, based on their own values, needs and priorities, a lack of - or very poor - political representation and a lack of access to social services.[8] In America, we conveniently forget Native Americans even exist.[9]

All People of Color are taught to avoid Black People and blackness if they want to be successful. The message is even more explicit when it comes to African Americans. With the acceptance of this deficit-based concept comes the illusion of powerlessness. It makes us more likely to see ourselves as helpless victims versus People who are being mistreated *and* have agency (power to) in our lives and communities. Within the American social hierarchy of Black People, African Americans (those who are descendants of African People brought to the United States as part of the transatlantic slave trade) have the lowest status.[10]

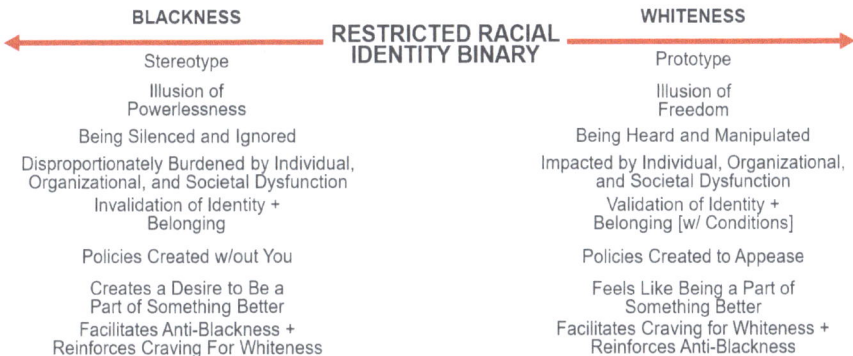

BLACKNESS	RESTRICTED RACIAL IDENTITY BINARY	WHITENESS
Stereotype		Prototype
Illusion of Powerlessness		Illusion of Freedom
Being Silenced and Ignored		Being Heard and Manipulated
Disproportionately Burdened by Individual, Organizational, and Societal Dysfunction		Impacted by Individual, Organizational, and Societal Dysfunction
Invalidation of Identity + Belonging		Validation of Identity + Belonging [w/ Conditions]
Policies Created w/out You		Policies Created to Appease
Creates a Desire to Be a Part of Something Better		Feels Like Being a Part of Something Better
Facilitates Anti-Blackness + Reinforces Craving For Whiteness		Facilitates Craving for Whiteness + Reinforces Anti-Blackness

Figure 9: Restricted Racial Identity Binary

When Black People (and people from other races and ethnicities who are considered People of Color) buy in to these ideas, any resemblance they have to blackness translates into lower status in the group. Colorism - the darker your skin, the lower your social status - is the most common manifestation of these ideas, but not the only one.

Human Irrationality Process: Why Ideas + Framing Matter

The ideas that have permeated American culture about People of Color in the form of stereotypes and expectations (or lack thereof) become the only lens through which we can *see* them. But it is not seeing People of Color at all. Whiteness facilitates comfort with a "colorblind" approach where White People and People of Color who have bought in to whiteness can pretend not to see People of Color. What they really see is a one-dimensional, partial picture of a human being. It is not only that stereotypes are false as a baseline for any Person of Color, but they are also blindingly obvious in their incompleteness. If you took all of the stereotypes about Black People for example, you would not end up with a complete person. That incomplete, dehumanized stereotype is what radiates through osmosis into the minds of all people in the United States and internationally thanks to colonization, media, the internet, and our collective acceptance.

My deeper exploration of racism, racial disparities, racial inequities, discrimination, and social injustices began personally. My husband and I have five children and are grateful and saddened that there are only two teenagers left in the house (this is me embracing complexity). Early in our relationship, we discussed the horrors of having to navigate as Black people in this society which has centuries of embedded ideologies that infect and shape us (although we did not quite have the ability to express it this way at the time). This system of ideas influences our thoughts on who we and other people are supposed to be, our interpersonal interactions, and our experiences with organizations and institutions (work, school, government, media, etc.). Although we did not have the language to fully understand why we had these experiences, we knew that we needed to learn them to be able to help our children thrive in a world that is not designed for them to do so.

Preprogrammed default settings prime us to more readily accept false concepts about BIPOC and White People. We have been programmed with a pattern of ideas that are not explicitly about racism but lay the foundation for the types of logical fallacies or flawed logic that pairs well with ideological racism. Although research has been used as a tool to justify oppression, whenever it gets close to uncovering any truths that get in the way of those in traditional power, there is a surge of anti-intellectualism,[11] a term coined by Richard Hofstadter which means a resentment and suspicion of experts and intellectuals, accompanied by a constant attempt to minimize their relevance through low-brow responses containing no or flawed logic which "gravely inhibit or impoverish intellectual and cultural life."[11]

As I was writing this book, I had an aha moment. I found a pattern between logical fallacies, cognitive bias, and cognitive distortions that was helpful to my own understanding and growth. I hope it is helpful to you as well. Before I get in to it, here is a brief overview of logical fallacies, cognitive bias, and cognitive distortions.

Logical fallacies are externally communicated errors in logic represented by false statements, arguments, or justifications. We communicate this flawed logic externally to other people or other people express them to us.

Cognitive bias is a systematic error in thinking that occurs when we are processing information and affects our decisions and judgments. They are not always negative; just our brain's attempt to simplify information processing so we do not get overwhelmed.[12] Biases often work as rules of thumb that help us make sense of the world and reach decisions with relative speed. However, they are not effective in dealing with the volatility, uncertainty, complexity, and ambiguity (VUCA) of people, situations, and organizations.

Cognitive distortions are exaggerated or irrational thought patterns. They fuel our negative inner voice that happens to be associated with the onset and perpetuation of mental health conditions like anxiety and depression. These inaccurate thoughts are ways that we can convince ourselves of something that isn't really true, a fantastic version of reality that usually reinforces negative thinking or emotions. Often our inner voice is telling us things that sound rational but only serve to keep us from feeling good about ourselves and other people.[13]

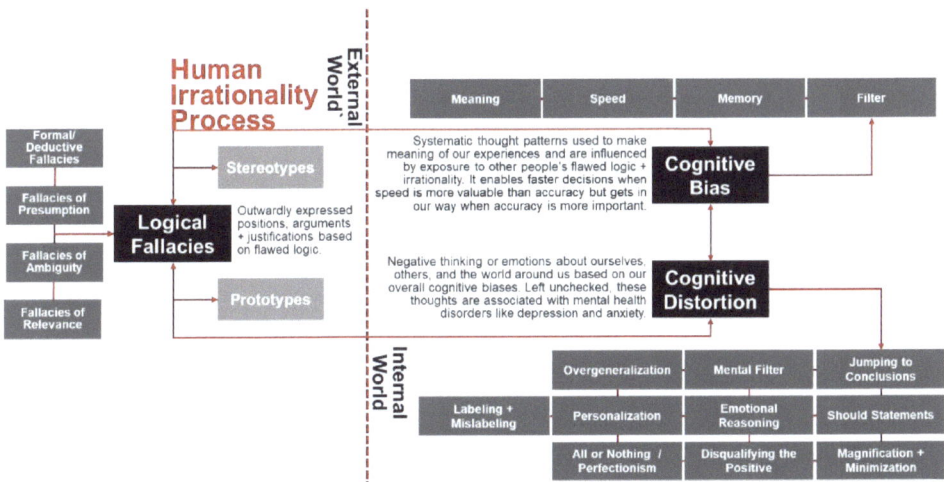

Figure 10: Human Irrationality Process (Detailed)

There are so many logical fallacies and cognitive biases that you could make an entire encyclopedia with multiple volumes. However, there are a particularly dangerous set of cognitive biases that fall into the category of cognitive distortions that have been associated with contributing to or worsening mental health disorders. These cognitive distortions are the drivers behind the logical fallacies we receive and communicate. The following is a list of common ideas that we use to distort the reality of ourselves, others, and the world around us.[13-15]

All-or-Nothing Thinking. This type of thinking involves viewing things in absolute terms. Everything is black or white, everything or nothing. If our performance falls short of perfect, we see ourselves or others as total failures. There is an inability or unwillingness to see shades of gray. In other words, we see extremes – something is either fantastic or awful. This type of thinking is reinforced by the popular narratives. There always has to be a hero, a victim, and a villain representing good and bad/evil. We frame people as either Republican or Democrat, white or black, rich or poor. And in this process, we dehumanize ourselves and each other. We are not either/or, we can hold many ideas and identities, and none of them are intrinsically good or evil. We all have done both good and bad, but that is not WHO we are; it is what we have done.

Overgeneralization. When we make a rule after a single event or a series of coincidences to create a pattern. Overgeneralizing can lead to overly negative thoughts about ourselves, others, and our environment based on only one or two experiences. This is most obviously represented when we encounter a White Person who has not started their racial equity journey and apply their behavior to all White People. Now, I know this is a hard one. I struggle with this because it is complicated. All White People have been exposed to socialization that impacts their beliefs and behavior AND All White People are not the same. Similarly, when we encounter a Person of Color who is doing something we do not like or agree with, we immediately use it as a point of data to reinforce stereotypes.

Mental Filter. When we take one small event and focus on it exclusively, filtering out anything else. Similar to overgeneralization, the mental filter distortion focuses on a single negative piece of information and excludes all the positive ones. The words "always" or "never" frequently appear in the sentence. This is related to a confirmation bias where we can only see the negative aspects of a person or situation.

Disqualifying the Positive. The "Disqualifying the Positive" distortion acknowledges positive experiences but rejects instead of embracing them. This is an especially vicious distortion since it can facilitate the continuation of negative thought patterns *even in the face of strong evidence to the contrary*. If we internalize the belief that all BIPOC are helpless people in need of saving, despite all evidence to the contrary, we do not really believe that we deserve to be in certain spaces (See Chapter 4 for more on Imposter Experience).

Jumping to Conclusions: We make negative interpretations even though there are no definite facts that support our conclusions. There are two types: **[1]** Mind Reading - This "Jumping to Conclusions" distortion manifests as the inaccurate belief that we know what another person is thinking. Of course, it is possible to have an idea of what other people are thinking. However, this distortion refers to arbitrarily concluding that someone is reacting negatively to us and we do not bother to find out. **[2]** Fortune Telling - A related distortion, fortune telling refers to the tendency to make predictions based on little-to-no evidence and holding them as gospel.

There is no way for us to know how things will turn out, but we see our predictions as fact rather than one of several possible outcomes. I have experienced this a lot in interactions with other Black People and People of Color as well as with White People. White People tend to assume that BIPOC are insinuating that they are racist – they might be. BIPOC tend to assume that a White Person's behavior is about them being BIPOC – of course this is a major possibility, but it can also be that someone just died, they are stressed out, or some combination of your suspicion and some other real-life challenges. In all cases, other people's thinking and behavior is rarely about us as people, but their perception of us. Their perception is not who we really are so the problem is not with us…they do not even know us.

Magnification (Catastrophizing) or Minimization: Also known as the "Binocular Trick" for its stealthy skewing of our perspective, this distortion involves exaggerating or minimizing the meaning, importance, or likelihood of things. This distortion is when we focus on a mistake or situation and make it out worse than it really is. It can show up as disregarding someone's concern about an offensive, racially charged statement as just being a joke. It can also be used to amplify and reinforce stereotypes and prototypes by exaggerating their significance in how we see ourselves, others, and situations.

Emotional Reasoning: This may be one of the most surprising distortions, and it is also one of the most important to identify and address because of its widespread impact. Emotional reasoning refers to the acceptance of our emotions as fact. It can be described as *"I feel it, therefore it must be true."* Just because we feel something does not mean it is true. If we feel threatened, it does not mean that someone else threatened us, but we interpreted the situation in a way that caused us to feel threatened. The goal is to explore why we felt that way. It may be justified or not, but our feelings are reactions not reality. This is also important when we are faced with cognitive dissonance (more details are later in this chapter). The feelings of discomfort we have when faced with our own internal conflict can lead to emotional reasoning that prevents us from learning and growing.

Should Statements: Another particularly damaging distortion is the tendency to make "should" statements. "Should" statements are statements that we make to ourselves and others, imposing a set of expectations that will likely not be met. When we hang on too tightly to our "should" statements about ourselves, the result is often guilt that we cannot live up to them. When we cling to our "should" statements about others, we are generally disappointed by their failure to meet our expectations, leading to anger and resentment. This is closely related to objectivity as a major characteristic of oppression. We place expectations associated with whiteness and anti-blackness on others in a way that supports their dehumanization. We have to be careful not to place "should" statements on ourselves based on external stereotypical and prototypical expectations.

Labeling and Mislabeling: These tendencies are extreme forms of overgeneralization, in which we assign judgments of value to ourselves or to others based on one instance or experience. Mislabeling refers to the application of highly emotional, loaded, and inaccurate or unreasonable language when labeling. For example, a Native American woman who labels herself as "an utter fool" for failing an assignment is engaging in this distortion. Another example is the Asian manager who labels an employee "an angry Black Woman" because the manager wanted to touch her hair but the employee refused the request.

Personalization: This is when we take everything personally or assign blame to ourselves without logical reason. This distortion covers a wide range of situations, from when a White Person assumes that people are calling them racist when they provide insight into the lack of diversity in leadership, to the more severe examples of believing that we as BIPOC are the cause for all negative emotions in others around us. A common form of personalization I have experienced is when people who offend BIPOC or have the traditional power to fix specific problems affecting BIPOC want to remind us of how much they care, all that they have done, and why they are offended that we do not appreciate them. Their feelings and intentions trump their impact: BIPOC pain, suffering and, in many cases, death. The personalization distortion distracts us from our power to address real issues in people's lives and our organizations by making it about ourselves.

Control Fallacies: A control fallacy manifests as one of two beliefs: (1) that we have no control over our lives and are helpless victims of fate, or (2) that we are in complete control, giving us responsibility for the feelings of those around us. Both beliefs are damaging, and both are equally inaccurate. No one is in complete control of what happens to them, and no one has absolutely no control over their situation. Even in extreme situations where we seemingly have no choice in what we do or where we go, we still have a certain amount of control over how we approach the situation mentally.

Fallacy of Fairness: While we would all probably prefer to operate in a world that is fair, the assumption of an inherently fair world is not based in reality and can foster negative feelings when we are faced with proof of life's unfairness. A person who judges every experience by its perceived fairness has fallen for this fallacy, and will likely feel anger, resentment, and hopelessness when they inevitably encounter a situation that is not fair.

Fallacy of Change: Another 'fallacy' distortion involves expecting others to change if we pressure or encourage them enough. This distortion is usually accompanied by a belief that our happiness rests on other people, leading us to believe that forcing those around us to change is the only way to get what we want. In racial equity and social justice work, it is easy to fall into the trap of trying to *make* people change. That is a delusion we need to let go of. What we can do is set clear expectations for how people engage with us; model the behavior we expect; and support people in organizations with knowledge, skills, and tools for how we do our work and hold them accountable to it.

Always Being Right: Perfectionists and those struggling with Imposter Syndrome will recognize this distortion. For those struggling with this distortion, the idea that we could be wrong is absolutely unacceptable, and we will fight to the metaphorical death to prove that we are right. It is not simply a matter of a difference of opinion, it is an intellectual battle that must be won at all costs. This is how many conversations go, whether they are related to racism or not.

Heaven's Reward Fallacy: This distortion is a popular one, and it's easy to see many examples of this fallacy playing out on big and small screens across the world. The "Heaven's Reward Fallacy" manifests as a belief that our struggles, suffering, and hard work will result in a just reward. How many examples can you think of in your life where hard work and sacrifice did not pay off? Sometimes no matter how hard we work or how much we sacrifice, we will not achieve what we hope to. To think otherwise is a potentially damaging pattern of thought that can result in disappointment, frustration, anger, and even depression when the awaited reward does not materialize.

Throughout this book, I regularly refer to the concept of whiteness or what is called white supremacy culture. One of the most referenced resources I have seen is *Dismantling Racism: A Workbook for Social Change Groups* by Kenneth Jones and Tema Okun. These characteristics are aligned with patterns of oppression for which many thought leaders have provided frameworks to help us better recognize and disrupt them such as Lee Anne Bell,[16] Hardiman, Jackson, and Griffin,[17] and Paolo Freire.[18] See the table on the following page for how the qualities of oppression align with the characteristics of whiteness. These are key concepts that reinforce racism in our interactions and organizations. Although the traits of whiteness are the opposite of thinking and behavior that is healthy (in terms of ego functioning or resilience – see the previous chapter), I have not done research on determining if this is a chicken or egg situation. In other words, why did these traits occur: has White dominant/elite culture always been this way **OR** are these the outcomes of structuring societies in such oppressive ways? Regardless, I want you to think about the cognitive distortions you just read and review the following table.

Figure 11: Qualities of Oppression + Traits of Whiteness

Qualities of Oppression	Description	Characteristics of Whiteness*
Exploitation	Having a scarcity mindset that facilitates conscious and unconscious fear, competition, transactional approaches, and mistreatment of individuals or groups resulting in unearned benefits and an unjust return on investment/contribution	➲ Individualism ➲ Progress is Bigger, More ➲ Sense of Urgency
Exclusion	A situation in which a person or group is baselessly prevented from or questioned about being present in a space, taking part in activities, doing their work, having knowledge/expertise, or having their needs truly be considered and addressed	➲ Worship of the Written Word ➲ Quantity Over Quality ➲ Perfectionism
Powerlessness	Not being able to see or tap into people's individual or collective strength or resources because it is assumed that there is a lack of knowledge, authority/influence, or capabilities to act	➲ Power Hoarding ➲ Paternalism ➲ I'm the Only One
Burden	The disproportionate bearing of painful and oppressive experiences or impacts that often go unacknowledged or are disregarded	➲ Fear of Open Conflict ➲ Defensiveness ➲ Right to Comfort
Objectivity	The false belief that we can deal with people or situations without distortion from personal feelings, cognitive bias, or interpretations	➲ Objectivity ➲ Only One Right Way ➲ Either/Or Thinking

*I will explain why I mapped certain characteristics of whiteness to these qualities of oppression on IntentionallyAct.com...please hold me accountable to this.

Cognitive distortions are woven into the systemic ways of thinking listed in the table above. The list of cognitive distortions aligned with many of the ways of thinking associated with American ideals, whiteness, and antiblackness. Furthermore, the qualities of oppression and whiteness are the opposite of healthy ego functioning and resilience. The warped perspectives about who People of Color and White People are supposed to be are literally making us sick. They are barriers to us having a worldview that aligns with reality and a healthy inner narrative.

Cognitive Dissonance + Learning

Cognitive dissonance is when what we believe is in conflict with what we do or have done. It causes us to have inner conflict and mental discomfort. There are three main causes of cognitive dissonance:

- **Forced Compliance.** Sometimes we find ourselves doing things that are opposed to our own beliefs because of external expectations, often for work, school, or a social situation.[1] This might involve going along with certain racist ideas due to peer pressure or not speaking up about racist statements or policies at work because we are worried about getting fired.
- **New Information.** Sometimes learning new information can lead to feelings of cognitive dissonance. For example, if you engage in a behavior that you later learn is harmful, it can lead to feelings of discomfort. People sometimes deal with this either by finding ways to justify their behaviors or to discredit or ignore new information.
- **Decisions.** People make decisions on a daily basis. When faced with two similar choices, people often are left with feelings of dissonance because both options are equally appealing. Once a choice has been made, however, people need to find a way to reduce these feelings of discomfort. People accomplish this by justifying why their choice was best so that they can believe that they made the right one.

The degree of discomfort we feel depends on two main factors. The first is the importance that we give to the belief being challenged. The more personal or sacred the belief is to our sense of self, the more discomfort we feel. With racism, many of the ideas we have internalized have been subtly tied to our identity. The second factor is the number of beliefs that are being challenged at the same time. The more clashing thoughts that we have, the greater the feelings from the inner conflict. It does not just influence how we feel. It motivates us to take action to reduce feelings of discomfort, which can be productive or unproductive. Some of the ways we may cope with these feelings include:

- Adopting beliefs or ideas to help justify the conflict between our beliefs or behaviors. This can sometimes involve blaming other people or outside factors.
- Hiding our beliefs or behaviors from other people. We may feel ashamed of our conflicting beliefs and behaviors, so hiding the disparity can help minimize feelings of shame and guilt.
- Only seeking out information that confirms our existing beliefs. This phenomenon, known as the confirmation bias, affects the ability to think critically about a situation but helps minimize feelings of dissonance.
- Change our beliefs or behavior to align with the new information, who we thought we were, or who we want to be.

We like to believe that we are logical, consistent, and good at making decisions. Cognitive dissonance can interfere with the perceptions we hold

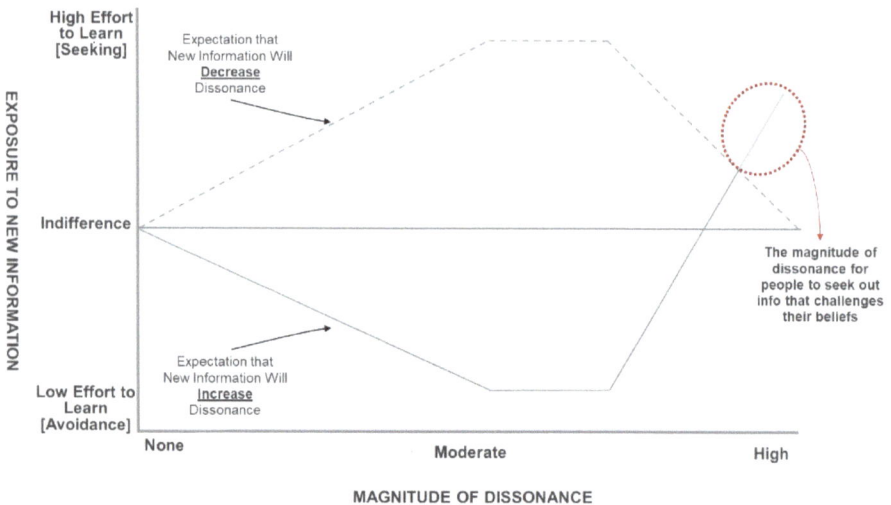

Figure 12: Relationship between Magnitude of Dissonance and Active Exposure to New Information

about ourselves and our abilities, which is part of the reason why it can often feel so uncomfortable and unpleasant. The discomfort can motivate us to defend, deny, and justify.

The self-justification necessary to defend our mistakes is a waste of energy, emotions, and time. However, cognitive dissonance is a powerful motivator for us to justify thoughts, attitudes, and beliefs that are not aligned with who we think we are. When our self-perception collides with our actions, they are considered dissonant in relation to each other. Whether the source of the discrepancy is our behavior, feelings, opinions, observations in the environment, they can be changed: We can change our opinions and behavior, as well as distort our perceptions and the information about the world around us. However, the higher the level of mental discomfort we experience, the more likely we can be open to or seek out information that will contradict the ideas we held.[19] The changes we make that create or restore consistency are referred to as dissonance-reducing changes.[20]

When racial equity and social equity educational experiences are designed well, they channel the discomfort of cognitive dissonance into a healthy set of intentional actions that offer a way out. We can facilitate true learning by helping people build their knowledge, reinforcing it through experiences that help us to internalize the knowledge, and developing skills through deliberative practice.[21]

Disruptors of Ideological Racism: Change Consciousness

How to Shift Our Thought Patterns. We have the opportunity to change our reactions to our environment. This creates the space over time for us to change the dynamics of our environment. The process starts with self-awareness, but it is something we are all able to do with sustained learning and effort. The ABC Model of Resilience works in part by clarifying this connection between our beliefs and our emotions. This clarity helps us to prevent the events around us from dictating if we show up as

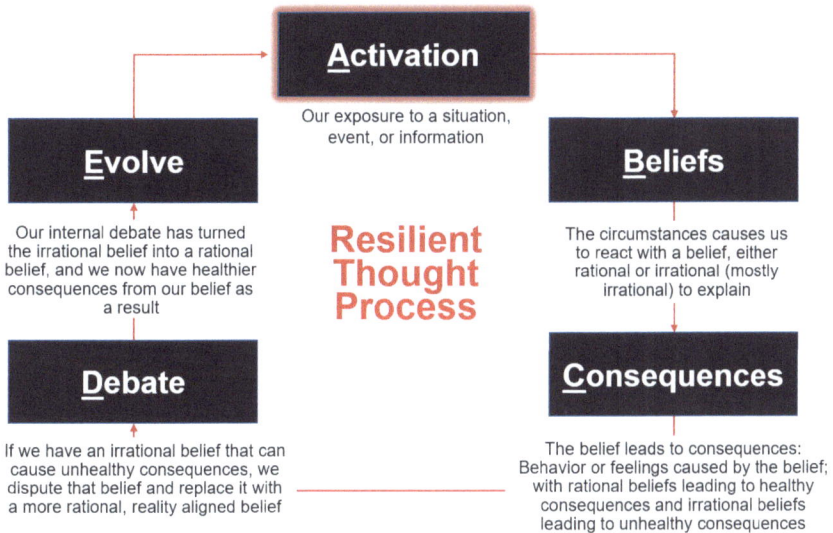

Figure 13: Resilient Thought Process

our best selves. I remixed the model a little bit in figure 13 to illustrate how it can support a more resilient thought process.

- ⇨ **Activation:** A situation, event, or information activates discomfort and starts a process where we create a story based on very little information.
- ⇨ **Beliefs:** The circumstances cause us to react with a belief based on the story we told ourselves, either rational or irrational (mostly irrational) to explain it. People's race plays a role in the stories we tell ourselves.
- ⇨ **Consequences:** The belief leads to consequences that show up as behavior or feelings caused by the belief. Our rational beliefs can lead to healthy consequences and irrational beliefs can lead to unhealthy consequences if we do not manage ourselves.
- ⇨ **Debate:** If we have an irrational belief that can lead to

unhealthy consequences, we dispute it and replace it with a more rational, reality aligned belief.

➲ **Evolve:** Once we have surfaced and debated our irrational beliefs, we can turn it into a more rational one, and we now can shift our thinking and behavior to achieve healthier consequences of our evolved belief.

The beginning of any real change process starts with shifting how we understand the root problem. Changing consciousness means learning about how and why we think and behave in ways that habitually support the limitations racism and other forms of oppression have placed on our identities, individual and collective. The goal is to build knowledge that clarifies our conductor/disruptor roles as individuals and organizations, how it plays out in society, and our opportunities to choose new ways of thinking and behaving.

In order to understand our social context, it is important to evaluate our current racial realities by exploring how psychology, neuroscience, and sociology influence our development, and the types of thinking and behavior that reinforce oppressive conditions. This chapter has begun the process; however, there is so much to learn.

Racial Equity Literacy. Part of the *so much more to learn* is deepening our understanding of how we got here. This includes exploring our historical context so we can connect our collective racial history to present-day inequities. Much of the history that helps us to understand where racism-reinforcing ideas come from is not a part of our traditional educational experiences. I have encountered people who have master's degrees in history who did not learn the complexity involved and different realities of BIPOC in the context of what they have learned. That is why books like *The Color of Law*,[22] *White Rage*,[23] *The Warmth of Other Suns*,[24] and *Stamped from the Beginning*[25] can shake us to our core: They reveal historical knowledge that we did not learn in school but we *thought* we knew. I am not proposing that we all need to become historians. However, if we are leading a change process to get ourselves and each other on a more transformative path to racial equity and our full human potential, then we are responsible for learning the historical context that directly impacts our lives, communities, organizations, and larger society.

The next step is to internalize what we have learned. What are our own underlying beliefs and habits that contribute to the system of racism? How does new historical information clarify current realities? For you? For your neighborhood? For issues that impact your work/career?

Critical Thinking. The ability to make decisions based on a reliable process is a vital skill in the modern world. The need for critical thinking is necessary in many different contexts. It is particularly important to be a disruptor of the ideas that reinforce racism. Why? Because each and every one of us thinks. However, the majority of our thinking is biased, self-serving, group-centered, uninformed, and unconscious. Our ability to reach our full human potential is heavily influenced by the quality of our thought. Therefore, our ability to fight the problematic ideas of racism demand that we step up our thinking game. When we are lazy in our thinking we are likely acting as conductors of oppression.

Critical thinking is the practice of improving the quality of our thinking by applying skills to decrease the likelihood of falling in to flawed logic and applying critical analysis and reflection. When combined with the personal competencies of emotional intelligence, critical thinking supports our resilience to oppression, especially the ideological layer of oppression.

Although we say that critical thinking is an important part of education, it is rarely achieved in secondary or higher education. There has been research that shows us not only is it possible to learn critical thinking approaches, but people can retain the learning and apply these skills in different contexts.[26]

Emotional Intelligence and Communication. These skills for disruptors support the following list of resilience factors:

- ⮫ **Self-Awareness.** Being able to effectively manage our feelings and impulses in a healthy manner. *Knowledge + Skills for Disruptors: Emotional Intelligence + Racial Equity Literacy*
- ⮫ **Agency + Self Direction:** Having the capacity to make realistic plans and to carry them out. Having an internal locus of control. *Knowledge + Skills for Disruptors: Critical Thinking + Racial Equity Literacy*
- ⮫ **Self-Esteem:** Our ability to have a good self-image is earned through building confidence in our strengths and abilities as well as knowing our limitations. *Knowledge + Skills for Disruptors: Communication + Racial Equity Literacy*
- ⮫ **Inner Narrative:** This internally driven cognitive dissonance is heightened by internalizing the ideas of whiteness and antiblackness. We want to be good people and the thought that we are contributing to the system of racism translates in our minds to being a bad person. As a Black, Indigenous, or Person of Color these ideas can have us constantly questioning ourselves, our interactions, and people who look like us. This is not usually a conscious process, but we can surface these thoughts and shift them. *Knowledge + Skills for Disruptors: Communication + Critical Thinking + Racial Equity Literacy*
- ⮫ **Worldview**: Ideological racism shapes our worldview which shapes how we understand ourselves and the world around us. A

45

healthy worldview leads to a more sophisticated understanding of ourselves, others, and how things work. *Knowledge + Skills for Disruptors: Communication + Critical Thinking + Racial Equity Literacy*

Racial equity literacy, emotional intelligence (self-awareness), communication (intrapersonal), and critical thinking allow us to embrace the nuances of life and reduces the likelihood we will be lulled into complacency when we are confronted with irrational ideas about who BIPOC and White People are supposed to be or the way the world works. There is no easy way out of this. The only way to keep ourselves on the disruptor of oppression track is to go through it…not around, over, or under it. The struggle through the discomfort of cognitive dissonance and building our power within is an ongoing process that yields a type of resilience that no one can take from us.

I have not gone into detail on building the skills for disruptors of racism and other forms of oppression. A book is not the best vehicle for skill-building. However, if you would like to learn more and be a part of a learning community focused on building knowledge and skills to advance racial equity and build resilience, please join IntentionallyAct.com… it is free.

Chapter 3. Ideological: Cultivating the Craving

1.   Miller AN, Harris TM. Communicating to Develop White Racial Identity in an Interracial Communication Class. *Communication Education.* 2005/07/01 2005;54(3):223-242. doi:10.1080/03634520500356196

2.   Gorski PC. Cognitive dissonance as a strategy in social justice teaching.(Promising Practices). *Multicultural Education.* 2009;17(1):54.

3.   Covey SR. *7 Habits of Highly Effective People: Powerful Lessons in Personal Change.* Simon & Schuster; 2013.

4.   Van Wormer K, Besthorn FH. *Human Behavior and the Social Environment, Micro Level: Groups, Communities, and Organizations.* Third ed. Oxford University Press; 2017.

5.   Allen TW. *The Invention of the White Race.* vol I: Racial Oppression and Social Control. Verso; 2012.

6.   Allen TW. *The Invention of the White Race.* vol II: The Origin of Racial Oppression in Anglo-America. Verso; 2012.

7.   Brondolo E, Libretti M, Rivera L, Walsemann KM. Racism and social capital: The implications for social and physical well-being. *Journal of Social Issues.* 2012;68(2):358-384. doi:10.1111/j.1540-4560.2012.01752.x

8.   United Nations. Let's Fight Racism: Indigenous Peoples. Department of Global Communications. Accessed 9/19/2020, 2020. https://www.un.org/en/letsfightracism/indigenous.shtml

9.   Obomsawin M. The Myth of Native American Extinction Harms Everyone. Boston Globe Media Partners. Accessed 9/19/2020, 2020. https://www.bostonglobe.com/2020/09/15/magazine/myth-native-american-extinction-harms-everyone/?p1=Article_Feed_ContentQuery

10.   Greer CM. *Black Ethnics: Race,Iimmigration, and the Pursuit of the American Dream.* Oxford University Press; 2013.

11.   Hofstadter R. *Anti-Intellectualism in American Life.* Vintage Books A Division Random House; 1962.

12.   Ross HJ. *Everyday Bias: Identifying and Navigating Unconscious Judgements in Our Daily Lives.* Rowman & Littlefield Publishing Group, Inc.; 2014.

13.   Burns D. *Feeling Good: The New Mood Therapy.* Collins, An Imprint of HarperCollins Publishers; 1980.

14.   PositivePsychology.com. Cognitive Distortions: When Your Brain Lies to You. Accessed 11/7/2020, https://positivepsychology.com/cognitive-distortions/

15.   Beck AT. *Cognitive Therapy and the Emotional Disorders: A Major Exploration of an Influential Approach to the Understanding and Treatment of Mental Illness.* International Unversities Press; 1979.

16.   Bell LA. Theoretical Foundations for Social Justice Education. In: Adams M, Bell LA, Griffin P, eds. *Teaching for Diversity and Social Justice.* Routledge; 1997:3-15:chap 1.

17.   Hardiman R, Jackson BW, Griffin P. Conceptual Foundations for Social Justice Education. In: Adams M, Bell LA, Griffin P, eds. *Teaching for Diversity and Social Justice*. Third ed. Routledge; 2007:3-15:chap 3.

18.   Freire P. *Pedagogy of the Oppressed*. Bloomsbury; 1970:183.

19.   Festinger L. *A Theory of Cognitive Dissonance*. Stanford University Press; 1957.

20.   Festinger L. Cognitive Dissonance. *Scientific American*. 1962;207(4):93. doi:10.1038/scientificamerican1062-93

21.   Brown PC, Roediger HL, McDaniel MA. *Make It Stick: The Science of Successful Learning*. The Belknap Press of Harvard University Press; 2014.

22.   Rothstein R. *The Color of Law: A Forgotten History of How Our Government Segregated America*. Liveright Publishing Corporation, a division of W.W. Norton & Company; 2017.

23.   Anderson C. *White Rage: The Unspoken Truth of Our Racial Divide*. Bloomsbury USA, an imprint of Bloomsbury Publishing Plc; 2016.

24.   Wilkerson I. *The Warmth of Other Suns: The Epic Story of America's Great Migration*. Random House; 2011.

25.   Kendi IX. *Stamped From the Beginning: The Definitive History of Racist Ideas in America*. Nation Books; 2016.

26.   Holmes NG, Wieman CE, Bonn DA. Teaching critical thinking. *Proceedings of the National Academy of Sciences of the United States of America*. 2015;112(36):11199-11204.

4. INTERNALIZED: DEVELOPING THE CUES WITHIN US

It is a peculiar sensation, this double consciousness, this sense of always looking at one's self through the eyes of others. – W.E.B. Du Bois
Concern should drive us into action and not into a depression. No person is free who cannot control themselves. – Remix of Pythagoras

Our human default settings are the canvas on which the ideas that support the system of racism are painted. The final masterpiece of ideology traps us within an unquestioned set of beliefs, attitudes, preferences, and actions. We assume that these ideas are the ultimate truth. They tell us the *right* way to conduct ourselves, how we should do things, and what we should expect from others.

The direct and indirect ideas of racism described in the previous chapter have been deeply seeded in all of us. As we inadvertently go through a learning process, the infection of these ideas embeds itself just like a biological or computer virus: whether we want them to or not...whether we believe in them or not. Internalized racism is the mostly unconscious acceptance of the dehumanizing attitudes, values, standards and the opinions of others into our own identity or sense of self. The conformity to these accepted ideas is reinforced through our interactions with other people and organizations.

I began professionally exploring racism and social injustices through the lens of law enforcement and emergency management. After the military, I worked in federal and local law enforcement as an analyst. I analyzed and visualized data, wrote reports, and noticed the disparities and attitudes associated with underestimated members of our communities. I was fascinated by how seemingly thoughtful and nice people could be lulled into such irrational and inhumane thinking and behavior. It started me on a path to better understand what seemed to be such contradictory states of existence in the same human being. At this point I began to evolve my studies beyond what racism was to how it worked.

This curiosity led me to focus my master's thesis and Doctoral research on socially vulnerable populations and how they disproportionately bore the burden of emergencies and disasters. By this point I was working in emergency management and later public health preparedness (the public health arm of emergency management) and had been dubbed a pracademic by a colleague in. As the nation had begun to reconcile with the volumes of research and reports highlighting the failures of Hurricane Katrina, I sensed that there was a difference by race, but the research was profoundly jarring to me and helped me realize my own social conditioning. In writing up my research for my degrees, I felt a sinking feeling every time I had to discuss race or racism. At this time, there was not very much public discourse on these issues, and I had never explicitly named it outside the walls of my home or in the company of other Black, Indigenous, or other People of Color (BIPOC). Now I needed to understand why it was so hard for me to write about these issues. While publishing work is vulnerable, as it opens the door to critique, I knew a lot of my apprehension was really about the fact that I was discussing racism in a field that was not willing or ready to do so.

I had been to so many workshops on racism focused on White People being the ones uncomfortable with discussing racism or not fully comprehending it. However, here I was, a Black woman, and I was uncomfortable and struggling with my own understanding. This led me to a deeper exploration of internalized racism and oppression.

Learning is the process of acquiring knowledge and skills and having them readily available from memory so we can make sense of future problems and opportunities.[1] We tend to think of learning as only an intentional process. However, much of what we learn is not a conscious practice. Social expectations from family, friends, school, work, etc. are often an unconscious, subtle learning process mostly reinforced by repetition, rewards, and punishment. We often do not connect the dots between how we behave, where we learned the behavior, and how we are rewarded for conforming or punished for not conforming.

In 1983, Howard Gardner proposed that there was not just one type of intelligence, but eight modalities through which intelligence can capture the broader range of our human potential. Two of them have been classified as personal intelligence: intrapersonal and interpersonal.[2] In this chapter, we will focus on intrapersonal intelligence. Interpersonal intelligence will be discussed in Chapter 5.

The Habits of Internalized Racism

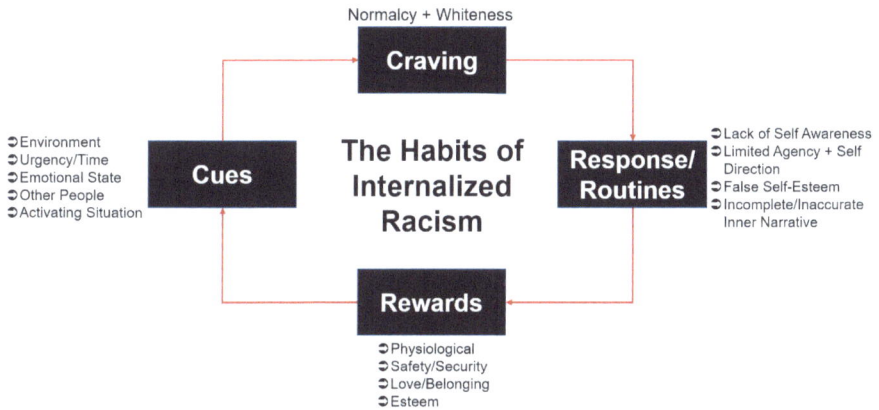

Normalcy + Whiteness

Craving

Cues
- Environment
- Urgency/Time
- Emotional State
- Other People
- Activating Situation

The Habits of Internalized Racism

Response/ Routines
- Lack of Self Awareness
- Limited Agency + Self Direction
- False Self-Esteem
- Incomplete/Inaccurate Inner Narrative

Rewards
- Physiological
- Safety/Security
- Love/Belonging
- Esteem

Figure 14: The Habits of Internalized Racism

Our ability to decide on our settings is directly related to emotional intelligence, particularly self-awareness and self-management. The more uncritically accepted default settings we have, the more ideologies of racism can permeate our consciousness and drive us. When we do not have a strong sense of self ("power within"), we are easily swayed to live the way other people expect us to.

We become what we think about most. Our success or failure in anything depends on our programming, what we accept from others, and what we say when we talk to ourselves. An understanding of the incredible function of the human brain has been missing from most of our attempts at growth. We are trying to force the brain to do things it is not designed to do. The reason why some people thrive more than others is because we were programmed differently from the beginning or worked to reprogram ourselves. Neither luck nor desire has anything to do with it.

It makes no difference whether we consciously believe it or not. The brain simply believes what you tell it and what it gets exposed to the most. What we tell it about ourselves it will create. Our brain is dependent on conditioning, the programming we receive from others, and on the conditioning, we subsequently accepted and kept giving ourselves. It is virtually impossible for us to do anything without that programming influencing us. Every thought and action are tied to beliefs that we have stored in our subconscious mind. Most of the programming we have received is in direct contradiction to what helps us thrive.

The narrative of who and how we are supposed to be, based on social norms from others, shapes our self-image. In time, we began to believe that what we are told by others and what we have told ourselves is true. What we could not do and could not accomplish. Repetition is a convincing argument. Eventually, we believe what people have told us and begin to live out the picture of what we have created in our minds. In time, we become what we believe most about ourselves. Unless we erase and replace that programming, we will be stuck with this the rest of our lives.[3]

What is the point? Racism and other forms of oppression systemically program each of us to think and behave in habitual ways that limit our own knowledge, development, and independence. It creates an individual and collective unconsciousness, a sort of mindlessness where we say and do things that we think are our own original positions but have been planted in us long ago and over time. Despite our uniqueness, certain predictable thinking and behaviors tend to arise because of our social programming.

White People have been taught that they have to strive for normalcy, to be complacent with the prototype of normalcy that someone else defined for them. In the same way People of Color have been taught that they too have to strive for this normalcy, but to do so in a world that will constantly remind you to that you are **ab**normal, a stereotype, a caricature of a human being. In the process, we are both striving for the concept of whiteness disguised as normal that no one can actually achieve and still reach their full human potential – because it requires each of us to give up our full humanity and self-determination.

And once you buy-in, consciously or unconsciously, life is supposed to be easier, more comfortable. And when it is not comfortable, we are even more prone to reinforce systems of oppression by blaming other people, usually people who are oppressed. If we all just go with the program, then we do not have to do the painstaking and exhilarating work of customizing our human default settings to ward off this social programming. The amazing thing about being human is our capacity to learn, grow, and evolve: To decide for ourselves who we want to be and act accordingly, in spite of the pull of unhealthy societal standards. Becoming who we want to be, accepting complexity and change, and recognizing our interdependence with others is a process Carl Jung called *Wholeness of Personality*; Nietzsche called it *Harmonious Totality,* Abraham Maslow called it *Self-Transcendence,* Robert Kegan called it *Self-Transforming.* .I use language similar to Paulo Freire: *Full Humanity*.

The irony to me is that the oppressive conditions in organizations and communities that are harmful to People of Color and other underestimated groups, are harmful for everyone else, too. The problems disproportionately impacting underestimated groups in our businesses, nonprofits, and government organizations, are the same ones that are harmful to any human being. However, it is worse for those of us who fall into those groups because of the historical and social context of oppression. Therefore, understanding the dynamics of oppression and shifting them contributes to making life better for all of us. There is no persona or social identity (progressive; social justice warrior; diversity, inclusion, and equity practitioner; philanthropy; organization awarded for diversity efforts, etc.) that can shield us from our responsibility to the continuous process of learning, adjusting, and strategic and informed action necessary to pursue our full potential as people and organizations.

We do not have to be at the mercy of the old programming that was never installed by us in the first place. We can begin to live up to the unlimited potential each of us was born with because we can take control of our thinking and behavior.

Whiteness has been taught to us without us even knowing it. Marketers tell us all the things we should own to be "normal," define what success should look like, and dictate what we should buy, and which holidays we should celebrate to be a real American. Politicians tell you everything we should believe about issues and how we should think in order to be accepted within whichever political party we belong. Organizations (intentionally and unintentionally) develop cultures that prescribe exactly how you should behave in order to belong so you can be a good fit.

BIPOC and White People are communicated the same messages that derail any sense of self and value rooted in our culture we may have or be trying to attain or maintain. **The same ideas upheld by people and institutions that are dangerous for BIPOC are also dangerous to White People.**

It should be noted though that the impacts are different and the outcomes exponentially worse for BIPOC because of racism's intergenerational history of policies, practices, and culture that have consistently been harmful, even deadly.

In *Pedagogy of the Oppressed*, Paulo Freire explains that people who are oppressed see themselves through the ideas that reinforce the system of oppression and as such become an extension of that system.[4] Internalization of whiteness and anti-blackness shows up in many ways for People of Color.

Imposter experience is also referred to as imposter syndrome. However, my preferred term is imposter experience due to how often so many people experience it, especially Black, Indigenous, and People of Color (BIPOC) and other underestimated groups.

An example is imposter experience, a common human experience that is especially prevalent for BIPOC. The negative messages about who we are supposed to be is overwhelming. These negative messages become intertwined with the positive messages about White People and the over-advertised, misleading perception that they have a monopoly on success. The majority of people at the height of various industries do not usually look like People of Color. The impact is that People of Color more frequently question whether we belong.

We often talk about shame when it comes to racism as an experience that only White People have. Shame refers to an "I am-ness." In guilt, the operating principle is that I have done something wrong; in shame the operating principle is, "I am something wrong." Part of the power of racism that becomes internalized in People of Color lies in the acceptance of the "I am something wrong" identity.[5] The key problem with the internalization of shame is that it creates cognitive dissonance with who we really are and who the world is telling us we are.

However, as we learn and grow, we begin to locate the seat of our decisions and identity within ourselves and as we navigate the world and others, we began to overcome the situations that limit us, we build a type of resilience. Let me be clear: **This is not about enduring racism, but about developing knowledge, skills, and tools that facilitate our agency (our ability to act) to fight the internalization of ideas and find others who we can partner with to shift the oppressive dynamics of this society.** Our ability to develop this 'power with' or influence through collective, strategic, and informed action exponentially increases impact on the underlying, systemic habits of racism in ourselves and the institutions/organizations that impact our lives.

Since People of Color have been exposed to the same ideas that White People have been exposed to about who we are supposed to be and who White People are supposed to be, we have the same infection that facilitates us also being passive conductors of the system of racism. Each one of us can recreate oppressive experiences and systems when we are not thinking consciously and acting intentionally. Oppression and conformity over time can transform each of us into passive **conductors** of oppressive systems like racism. However, there are major opportunities to think and behave in ways where we are proactive **disruptors** of oppression.

Yes, I know what some will say: "I am not willing to do the emotional labor of educating White People." I used to think that way too. Then I realized that I am already doing immeasurable amounts of emotional labor every day to survive and thrive despite racism. It stopped being about doing it for White People and became about using the power I have to shift the dynamics of my own experiences so I could reduce the emotional labor I was already exerting (including in dealing with people who are BIPOC).

Everyone has a different set of skills and abilities, so this looks different for each of us. Let's find our own voice in what this means for ourselves so we can build the habits to be disruptors of oppression for our own liberation as People of Color. Our work also includes how we think about ourselves, other People of Color, and White People. The infection of whiteness and subsequent craving means we have to examine and redefine who we are, what we stand for, what we tolerate, and how we advocate.

On the surface, whiteness, disguised as normal, has all the trappings of being part of something bigger than ourselves. It feels like something to

54

belong to that offers benefits many refer to as privileges. However, there is a trade-off: We have to conform to and condone standards, beliefs, and attitudes that we have not defined or analyzed for ourselves (see Chapter 3, Figure 3 for more information on the Restricted Racial Identity Binary). We never get to learn who we and other people are. It means superficial relationships and unfulfilling exchanges. Whiteness has become a default human setting. When are we going to customize these settings for ourselves? When do we get to decide: Who are you? What do you believe? Why? What do you want and need? What does success look like for you?

Our ability to see ourselves beyond the concept of whiteness and antiblackness, as a whole human being, is the reason we should all be motivated to confront racism and advance racial equity…not to save People of Color. As long as we do not see these within us, we cannot see how White People and People of Color are being hustled into a race to the bottom. The benefactors of the hustle are certainly not the common folks distracted by pursuit of whiteness and fighting amongst ourselves.[6] The people who benefit are those who hold the majority of the wealth and real power in America…the 1%. One percent of people who possess most of the income and wealth in the United States have seen their wealth grow by 187% since 1995 while the rest of us are lucky if we have seen our wealth grow by 7% since 1995.[7]

There is incredible danger in conformity, normality, and comfort: We do not do the hard work on ourselves and in our organizations to choose who we aspire to be and strive towards that vision. Psychologists, philosophers, cognitive scientists, social scientists, and many others have held that this work against conformity is the basis for increased mental health, creativity, productivity, and appreciation of ourselves not based on unhealthy societal standards/norms, but our own informed inner scorecard and effort.

Internalized racism for People of Color has been studied in academia, but much of this goldmine of information has remained in ivory towers. However, I have mapped identified patterns of internalized oppression[8] with the factors of resilience and healthy ego functioning (See Chapter 2) to show how the patterns negatively impact our lives, as documented in the following section.

Self-Awareness. Remember that self-awareness is our ability to understand our emotions in the moment and understand our tendencies across situations. These patterns of oppression disconnect us from our awareness of who we are and who we can be.

Table 1: Self-Awareness & Internalized Racism

Self-Awareness Pattern (Individual & Group)	Sources
Fear and terror [Variations: Fear of freedom, fear of own power and self-determination, fear of violence, fear of action against oppression]	Ahluwalia & Zegeye (2001); Brown (1995); Freire (1970); Love (2002); Miller (1986); Moane (1999); Morris (1987); Pharr (1996,1997); Tigert (1999)
Violence and abuse; Violence and destructiveness-- physical, emotional, verbal [Variations: Horizontal hostility, inter-group violence]	Dominick & Ebrahimi (2010); B. Duran & E. Duran (1995); Artz (1996); B. Duran & E. Duran (1995) Bobbe (2002); Freire (1970); Moane (1999); Pharr (1996); Tappan (2003); Tigert (1999, 2001); Young (1990)
Guilt [For not being more like stereotypes]	B. Duran & E. Duran (1995); Moane (1999)
Self-medicating and destructive or addictive behaviors [Alcohol, drugs, sex]	L. Brown (1986); B. Duran & E. Duran (1995); Moane (1999); Poupart (2003)
Inappropriate sexual behavior	L. Brown (1986); Moane (1999)
Anger, rage, hostility	J. Bell (2006); B. Duran & E. Duran (1995); Miller (1986); Moane (1999); Pharr (1996, 1997); Tigert (1999, 2001)
Lack of self- knowledge, distortion of self-knowledge	B. Duran & E. Duran (1995); Miller (1986); Moane (1999)
Loss and restriction of identity, history, culture, deculturalization, cultural estrangement	Moane (1999); Sonn & Fisher (1998, 2000)

Agency + Self-Direction. When we have agency and self-direction, we see ourselves as able to control key aspects of our environment and guide our behavior with purpose. We can engage in self-directed behavior, effectively guiding our actions toward goals across time, can manage impulses, and are resilient in the face of setbacks.

Table 2: Agency + Self Direction & Internalized Racism

Agency + Self-Direction Pattern (Individual & Group)	Source
Apathy, ambivalence, fatalism	Comas-Diaz, 1994; Freire, 1970; Moane, 1999; Morris, 1987
Belief in victimization status or sense	Brown (1995); Freire (1970); Love (2002)

Agency + Self-Direction Pattern (Individual & Group)	Source
of victimhood/suffering	
Failure to rebel, docility, compliance	Freire (1970); Love (2002); Morris ((1987); Pharr (1996,1997); Kasl (1992)
Helplessness/Learned helplessness	Ahluwalia & Zegeye (2001); B. Duran & E. Duran (1995); Comas-Diaz (1994); Love (2002); Moane (1999); Miller (1986); Morris (1987)
Lack of agency, and personal sense of no power, powerlessness	Ahluwalia & Zegeye (2001); J. Bell (2006); Comas-Diaz (1994); Joffe & Albee; Love (2002); Miller (1986); Moane (1999); Tigert (1999); Woolley (1993); Young (1990)
Lack of control	Love (2002); Tigert (1999)
Psychological and emotional dependence, lack of autonomy	Ahluwalia & Zegeye (2001); Freire (1970); Miller (1986); Moane (1999)

Self-Esteem. Self-esteem is closely related to agency. It is the extent to which we respect and value ourselves. Feeling good about ourselves, being able to accept our faults or limitations, and having self-compassion is disrupted by our internalization of oppression.

Table 3: Self-Esteem & Internalized Racism

Self-Esteem Pattern (Individual & Group)	Sources
Adequacy and competency	C. Brown (1995); Love (2002)
Arrogance	Moane, 1999
Care-taking/focus on needs and desires of dominant group [Variations: Mammification, placing dominant group's needs & Interests above your own]	Artz (1996); Love (2002); Miller (1986); Moane (1999); Morris (1987)
Deference to the dominant group [Variations: Submissiveness, passivity, docility]	Miller (1986)
Feelings of inferiority (self and group) and failure	Ahluwalia & Zegeye (2001); Comas-Diaz (1994); Love (2002); Miller (1986); Moane (1999); Pharr (1996); Tigert (1999,

Self-Esteem Pattern (Individual & Group)	Sources
	2001); B. Duran & E. Duran (1995); Miller (1986)
Feelings of insecurity	J. Bell (2006); Moane (1999)
Feeling ugly, evil, bad, unloved, or unwanted	J. Bell (2006); Comas-Diaz (1994); Miller (1986)
Low self-esteem, self-respect, self-worth and self- confidence, negative self-concept, self- doubt, self-blame, self- deprecation	Comas-Diaz (1994); Freire (1970); Hershel (1995); Joffe & Albee (1988); Miller (1986); Moane (1999); Morris (1987); Pharr (1996); Sonn & Fisher (1998, 2000); Tappan (2003); Woolley(1993)
Self-hatred [Individual and group]	B. Duran & E. Duran (1995); Moane (1999); Pharr (1996); Sonn & Fisher (2000)
Shame	Comas-Diaz (1994); B. Duran & E. Duran (1995); hooks (1995, 2001, 2002, 2004, 2005); Kaufman (1992); Bradshaw, (1988); Kaufman & Raphael (1996) Tigert, (1999, 2001)
Unwillingness to admit weakness or vulnerability	Miller (1986); Moane (1999)
Worthlessness, self- degradation	J. Bell (2006); L. Brown (1986); Freire (1970)

Relationship Management. A healthy ego makes it possible for us to have mutually satisfying relationships with others. The following impacts of internalized oppression damage the shared benefits we can get from relationships within and across racial and ethnic groups.

Table 4: Relationship Management & Internalized Racism

Relationship Management Pattern (Individual & Group)	Sources
Alienation	Bartky (1990); B. Duran & E. Duran (1995); Freire (1995); Hershel (1995); Love (2002)
Criticism and Invalidation	Dominick & Ebrahimi(2010)
Dissimulation (concealment of one's thoughts, feelings, or character; pretense.)	hooks (2005); Miller (1986); Moane (1999)

Attacking group leaders	B. Duran & E. Duran (1995); Pharr (1997)
Focus on individual empowerment/ individualism/ no group attachment	Love (2002); Pharr (1996, 1997)
Isolation and loneliness	C. Brown (1995); Love (2002) Moane (1999); Pheterson (1986); Tigert (1999)
Mutual distrust among group	Moane (1999)
Practice exclusion of other groups or members of own group	Dominick & Ebrahimi (2010); Love (2002)

Inner Narrative. Our inner narrative is the extent that our egos have an overarching and meaningful storyline that connects the different parts of ourselves together into a coherent story. The following impacts of internalization damage the stories we tell ourselves about who we are and who we can be.

Table 5: Inner Narrative & Internalized Racism

Inner Narrative Pattern (Individual & Group)	Sources
Attraction to and repulsion to dominant group	Fanon (1967, 1968); Freire (1970)
Collusion	B. Duran & E. Duran (1995); Morris (1987); Kirk & Okazawa-Rey (2007)
Contempt	Pharr (1996, 1997)
Desire to emulate dominant group	Freire (1970); Memmi (1965)
Duality [Individual, cultural, consciousness]	Du Bois (1995); B. Duran & E. Duran (1995); Fanon (1964, 1968); Freire (1970); Miller (1986); Moane 1999); Morris (1987); Young, (1990)
Hopelessness, Despair	J. Bell (2006); B. Duran & E. Duran (1995); Moane (1999); Woolley (1993)
Identify with those in power/dominant group	B. Duran & E. Duran (1995); Fanon (1967, 1968); Love (2002); Morris (1987); Pharr (1996); Tappan (2003)
Mental Illness and vulnerability to mental illness [Variations: Depression, PTSD, anxiety]	J. Bell (2006); Comas-Diaz (1994); B. Duran & E. Duran (1995); Moane (1999)
Panic, worry, urgency, hyper-criticalness	C. Brown (1995); L. Brown (1986); Moane (1999)

Inner Narrative Pattern (Individual & Group)	Sources
Restriction/modification of action	Moane (1999); Pharr (1997)
Unconscious application of internalized beliefs	B. Duran & E. Duran (1995); Jackins (1999); Love (2002); Morris (1987)
Internalization of negative group identities/oppressors' view of group	Fanon (1967, 1968); Freire (1970); Memmi (1965); Morris (1987); Sonn & Fisher, (1998, 2000); Young (1990)

Worldview. Our worldview is the degree of sophistication of our perspective, and the extent to which it provides us with a sense of direction toward what is real. The following internalized oppression patterns impact how we understand the world around us and create the boundaries or limitations for how we then see ourselves and other people.

Table 6: Worldview & Internalized Racism

Worldview Pattern (Individual & Group)	Sources
Preference for dominant group and things associated with it [Aesthetics (skin color, hair texture, Physical features), knowledge constructions]	Comas-Diaz (1994); Golden (2004); Love (2002); Russell, Midge, & Hall (1992)
Attribution of superiority of the dominant group [Variations: Competence; credibility, belief in invincibility, infallibility and/or magic of dominant group; mistrusting our thinking; love/hate paradox, envy/desire paradox]	Freire (1970); Hershel (1995); Lipsky (2006); Love (2002); Miller (1986);Tappan (2003)
Restriction of identity, no vision for alternate realities	Moane (1999); Pharr (1997)

External Realities. As a reminder, our external realities or network factors—our families, communities, organizations/institutions, and larger society—are important considerations because they are oftentimes not in our direct control. These external realities can be potential protective factors for, harmful to, or influenceable by our resilience. I categorize these patterns of internalization because the influence of the larger social context is a major contributor to them. No matter how resilient we are, there is a limited supply and external realities, like George Floyd, can pierce our resilience armor because we are only human.

Table 7: External Realities & Internalized Racism

External Realities Pattern (Individual & Group)	Sources
Feelings of being unsafe	C. Brown (1995); Love (2002)
Grief	B. Duran & E. Duran (1995); Moane (1999)
Humiliation	Moane (1999)
Inter-generational transmission of patterns, historical trauma	Brave Heart (1995, 1998, 2003); Braveheart-Jordan & Debruyn (1995, 1996, 1998); C. Brown (1995); Comas-Diaz (1994); B. Duran & E. Duran (1995) Love (2002); Pharr, (1996)
Physical symptoms of oppression [Physical ailments, suicide, substance abuse, destructive sexual behaviors,]	J. Bell (2006); L. Brown (1986); B. Duran & E. Duran (1995); Brave Heart (2003)

Although we often focus on how racism is internalized by People of Color, I would argue that many of these patterns of behavior are also seen in White People. When our sense of self is restricted at all levels of society by whiteness and antiblackness, the likelihood of personal and institutional dysfunction is high. The difference is that BIPOC are not extended any grace for our experiences or learned behavior; there is limited empathy or meaningful action.

In many cases, BIPOC are subjects of pity, a paternalistic position. Pity is more detached than compassion or empathy; we can pity people while maintaining a safe emotional distance from them.[9] While pity involves the belief in the inferiority of the person, compassion assumes equality in a common humanity. Pity involves implicit feelings and expressions of superiority: If I pity you, I think you are worse off than me, and thus, I am doing better than you. This hierarchy is a reason why healthy people never want to be the object of pity.[10]

Explanations focusing on BIPOC's social standing emphasize that the expression of racial bias in the form of discrimination deprives BIPOC of chances for social advancement. In contrast, explanations focusing on White People's social standing emphasize structural advantages and unearned privileges that afford Whites a disproportionate share of economic, cultural, social, and symbolic capital. Although White advantage and BIPOC disadvantage are often intimately connected (e.g. Black "disaccumulation" leading directly to White "accumulation"), White People's choice of interpretative frame can nonetheless profoundly affect their psychological experience of accepting social inequity. White People are more likely to support advancing racial equity if the focus is on BIPOC disadvantage.[11]

To see the complexity of racism, take Lyndon B. Johnson's saying: "If you can convince the lowest white man he's better than the best colored man, he won't notice you're picking his pocket. Hell, give him somebody to look down on, and he'll empty his pockets for you." Non-elite White People are being hustled by elite White People to focus their blame and attention on BIPOC.

Invisible Power: In the context of racism, invisible power is the way awareness of our rights and interests are hidden through the adoption of ideologies, values and forms of whiteness by Black, Indigenous, and Other People of Color (BIPOC). Sometimes this is also referred to as the 'internalization of powerlessness.' It affects our awareness and consciousness of potential issues, even though we are directly affected. We may be unaware of our rights, our ability to speak out, and we may come to see the thoughts, behavior, and outcomes of racism as natural, or at least unchangeable. Therefore, we do not question our situations and internalize a learned obliviousness, helplessness, and/or hopelessness. Experts and researchers tend to focus this concept on BIPOC or other underestimated groups in the context of different forms of oppression. However, we know that part of the insidiousness of racial oppression is that many White People who want to do the right thing also have invisible power. They do not know, cannot see, or are afraid of their power to take meaningful action. By influencing how we think about our place in the world, invisible power shapes our beliefs, sense of self, and acceptance of the status quo – even our own superiority or inferiority.

Strategies for challenging invisible power include awareness raising, adult education and skill building, participatory research to validate our own knowledge, uses of the media and popular communication methods to challenge racial stereotypes and narratives, changes in approaches to schooling and socialization, as well as many others. But hidden forms of power also can involve more hidden forms of action as well, in which we resist domination and control through less public ways. Just like dominating power can be exercised in hidden ways, so can strategies of opposition and resistance.

As a transition to discussing opportunities to purge ourselves of internalized whiteness and antiblackness, I would like to share a message from the great James Baldwin from *The Fire Next Time*. I highly recommend reading at least the first ten pages of this book (the section is called *My Dungeon Shook*). It is one of the most eloquent, moving, and real descriptions of the dynamics between BIPOC and White People.

> Please try to remember that what they believe, as well as what they do and cause you to endure, does not testify to your inferiority but to their inhumanity and fear. Please try to be clear…about the reality which lies behind the words *acceptance* and *integration*. There is no reason for you to try to become like white people and there is no basis whatever for their impertinent assumption that *they* much accept *you*. The really terrible thing old buddy, is that *you* must accept *them*. And I mean that very seriously. You must accept them and accept them with love. For these innocent people have no other hope. They are, in effect, trapped in a history which they do not understand; and until they understand it, they cannot be released from it. They have had to believe for many years, and for innumerable reasons, that black men are inferior to white men. Many of them, indeed, know better, but, as you will discover, people find it difficult to act on what they know. To act is to be committed, and to be committed is to be in danger. In this case, the danger, in the minds of most white Americans, is the loss of their identity.

The identity of White People that James Baldwin is referring to is not their ancestral ethnic or national origin. It is the social status granted to those who identify with whiteness and antiblackness. Baldwin did not get at this, but I am including BIPOC who knowingly and unknowingly align with whiteness and antiblackness in the category of those afraid of losing their identity.

Disruptors of Internalized Racism: Create a Vision + Choose Mindfulness

Now that we have a better understanding of (1) how we get infected by racism-reinforcing ideas; and (2) the underlying neuroscience and psychology. What do we do now?

We invest in building our power within starting with developing a clear image of (1) what it means to be a proactive disruptor of racism; and (2) what it looks like to have a proactively disruptive organizational culture. This includes building the resilience necessary to continuously advance racial equity. **Reader beware:** Our familiarity with the *right* language and having only an intellectual understanding of racism with no connection to our roles and responsibilities can create the illusion of being a disruptor of racism. The essence of advancing racial equity is owning our power to decide, commit to, and act upon who we really want to be, not which words we know.

Creating a strategic direction for ourselves requires a clear vision, mission, set of values, and goals for ourselves and/or our organizations that reflect how we would like to individually and collectively advance racial equity. Developing our strategic direction is our internally driven and externally lived commitment to a vision for who we would like to be as individuals and our collective identities for organizations.

One of the biggest challenges of the human journey is learning who we are, who we want to be, and managing ourselves to close the gap between the two. This challenge and responsibility are not limited to us as individuals. Organizations can create the space for (1) people to have the kind of **pro**fessional and **per**sonal (PROPER) development to understand themselves better and how that understanding is related to their goals and roles; and (2) developing and maintaining clear strategic direction (vision, mission, values, goals, etc.) that provides an anchor for employees' PROPER development and is embedded throughout the operations and habits of the organization.

In the previous chapter, we discussed challenging the ideas to which we have been exposed so we can change our consciousness. Now is time to reflect on those internalized lessons and follow our roadmap. Our vision or reimagined selves and organizations become our north star to guide our actions.

Chapter 4. Internalized: Developing the Cues Within Us

1.   Brown PC, Roediger HL, McDaniel MA. *Make It Stick: The Science of Successful Learning.* The Belknap Press of Harvard University Press; 2014.

2.   Behjat F. Interpersonal and intrapersonal intelligences: Do they really work in foreign-language learning? *Procedia - Social and Behavioral Sciences.* 2012/01/01/ 2012;32:351-355. doi:https://doi.org/10.1016/j.sbspro.2012.01.052

3.   Helmstetter S. *What to Say When You Talk to Yourself.* 2nd ed. Gallery Books; 2017:207.

4.   Freire P. *Pedagogy of the Oppressed.* Bloomsbury; 1970:183.

5.   Chapman RT. Internalized Racism of the Clinician and the Treatment Dynamic. *Journal of Emotional Abuse.* 2006;6(2-3):219-228. doi:10.1300/J135v06n02_13

6.   Glasberg SD, Shannon D. *Political Sociology: Oppression, Resistance, and the State.* Pine Forge, an Imprint of Sage Publications; 2011.

7.   Sawhill IV, Pulliam C. Six Facts about Wealth in the United States. Brookings Institute. Accessed 9/20/2020, 2020. https://www.brookings.edu/blog/up-front/2019/06/25/six-facts-about-wealth-in-the-united-states/

8.   Williams TK. Understanding Internalized Oppression: A Theoretical Conceptualization of Internalized Subordination. *Open Access Dissertations.* 2012;627

9.   Ben-Zeev A. Do Not Pity Me. Psychology Today. Accessed 11/14/2020, https://www.psychologytoday.com/us/blog/in-the-name-love/201008/do-not-pity-me

10.   Delft Institute of Positive Design. Pity. Delft University of Technology. Accessed 11/14/2020, https://emotiontypology.com/typology/list/pity

11.   Lowery BS. Framing inequity safely: Whites' motivated perceptions of racial privilege. *Personality & social psychology bulletin.* 2007;33(9):1237-1250.

5. INTERPERSONAL: THE DAILY ROUTINES OF RACISM

"The pursuit of full humanity, however, cannot be carried out in isolation or individualism, but only in fellowship and solidarity; therefore, it cannot unfold in the antagonistic relations between oppressors and oppressed. No one can be authentically human while...[they prevent]...others from being so."

-Paulo Freire, Pedagogy of the Oppressed

Interpersonal racism is the dehumanized ways we interact with each other based on the ideas we have been taught about who Black, Indigenous, and other People of Color (BIPOC) and White People are supposed to be. We all have been conditioned for a range of dysfunctional behaviors that perpetuates unhealthy relationships on top of which you add racism. For BIPOC, the incessant exposure to interactions that reinforce our objectification feels like a constant battle. There are too many scars on our health, wealth, and dignity. We are continuously being reminded of, and subjected to, what the world thinks it knows about us.

The impacts are real: Our quality of life, livelihood, and lives are on the line.[1, 2] Part of the process of racial oppression is the effort to obscure our pain, struggle, and power...we are not seen or heard because it is too uncomfortable for internalized whiteness. And if we are not seen or heard, it is almost impossible to be appreciated, valued, or respected. This is the reason activists fight so hard to get media attention...until the struggle is seen, it is as if it does not exist.[3] It is also why segregation by policy and by practice is held so tightly: Out of sight, out of mind. However, we are not victims. We are captains of our shabby ships that oppression dealt in the stormy seas of life. We can influence how we navigate and work together to get bigger and better boats to create our fleet of freedom.

For White People, the prototypes you have been exposed to do not allow your full identity to be expressed…you are given a paint by number image of yourself. You cannot go outside the lines, and you cannot get too crazy with the colors. At no point are you allow to mourn the loss of your history and culture that was sacrificed as a tradeoff for whiteness. Nor are you allowed to have a historical narrative outside of the pre-established immigrant story or heroic battles of your founding forefathers. A distorted historical perspective supersedes the historical reality because it does not fit the dominant whiteness narrative.

The level of identity restriction and dysfunctional behavior patterns that we all have internalized comes to a head when we interact with each other. In researching this book, I verified what I had long suspected: Our challenges with interpersonal racism are compounded by our challenges with interpersonal relationships. In this society, we are exposed to fictitious models of unhealthy relationships. Think across movie genres about the main themes: overcoming the monster (good versus evil), rags to riches, damsels in distress (referred to as rebirth), and so on. They feed us linear stories with limited character types, oversimplicity, and clear resolutions. These ideas have crossed the boundary from the external world into our inner worlds whether we want them to or not. Our brains have developed a lot of rules about people and the world based on fiction.

Having meaningful interactions with any other human being is built upon a foundation of the layers of our ego functioning and resilience: self-awareness, agency and self-direction, self-esteem, inner narrative, relationship management, worldview, and external realities (see Chapter 2). Without a strong foundation of the skills that support our interpersonal interactions, they will not be mutually beneficial, especially across races, ethnicities or any other type of differences. There are three main goals to interpersonal interactions that these skills support:

- ⮑ Gaining our Objective(s): We need skills to clarify what we want from the interaction and identifying what we need to do in order to get the results we want.
- ⮑ Maintaining Our Relationships: We need to understand how important the particular relationship is to us, how we want the person to feel about us, and what we need to do in order to maintain the relationship.
- ⮑ Keeping Our Self-Respect: We need intrapersonal and interpersonal skills to help us feel the way we would like to feel after the interaction is over and to stick to our values and to the truth.

The habits of interpersonal racism blur the lines of interpersonal interactions with racist ideas and behavior. Then we layer the unhealthy relationship dynamics we have been taught.

Habits of Interpersonal Racism

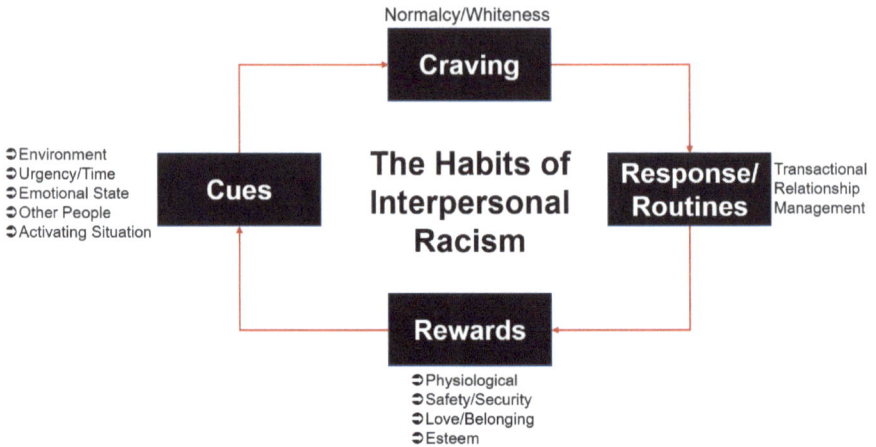

Figure 15: Habits of Interpersonal Racism

The most common experiences we have with each other is in workplaces. And through those interactions, you may have heard it before from colleagues (I have heard White People and BIPOC say this): I don't even see color. In fact, we all *see* color (as in race) and make judgments against BIPOC based solely on the information infection we have about who they are. We also make judgments against White People solely based on them being the bar of normalcy (prototype) for the rest of humanity. The reason we do not know that each of us contributes to the system of racism is because no one ever taught us to see it. There is no such thing as being colorblind…claiming it does not make it true. Furthermore, you are telling BIPOC that you do not see them, they should not see themselves, and as a result, you do not see yourself in relationship to them.[4]

There are many White People and People of Color that have tried to engage with someone else in a way that comes off as offensive. Instead of engaging with someone on a personal level from a place of curiosity and leaving some room for surprise, we engage with others as if they are only what we can identify with our eyes and all the associated assumptions.

For example, in formal settings, I have witnessed White People try to engage with me as if we were on some sitcom with the one Black neighbor whose words and behavior somehow represent me. It is as if they have been waiting so long to put into practice their vast knowledge from their deep study of Black People through the television and internet. In what feels to them like a genuine attempt to connect with me, they have insulted me and created a racially awkward situation. In most cases it has become comical, and I surface the hypocrisy with as much love as I can muster. For most

BIPOC (including me) it can become exhausting, painful, and anger inducing. It becomes a vicious cycle: White Person says or does something that is offensive, Person of Color speaks up and instead of the offensive statement being the subject and problem, the Person of Color becomes the problem for surfacing the offense.

In the workplace and other organizational settings, the same dynamic plays out. The White Person becomes the victim because they are offended that the Person of Color dared to voice their offense. The Person of Color then becomes the perpetrator because there is a White Person whose feelings are hurt. The human resources office is often a stop for the victimized White Person. People of Color, especially Black People, have lost their jobs for being "the angry Black Person" or someone felt "threatened." The needs of, concerns of, or harm to the Person of Color have no bearing on these situations.

In other workplace contexts, I have also been told during focus groups with clients that people have filed reports of racial discrimination that have created hostile work environments. However, the people that are problematic never suffer any consequences. Many People of Color know these experiences all too well and do not speak up because their livelihoods are on the line or they do not have the context, language, or practice to productively advocate for themselves in these kinds of situations.

It is true that White People can experience unpleasant interpersonal exchanges with People of Color because they are White…that is not reverse racism, that is interpersonal prejudice in action. History, attitudes, beliefs, behaviors, and organizations do not reinforce a deficit-based narrative about White People that supports the negative interaction to create a whole system of oppression that explicitly targets them thereby limiting their social, economic, and political access. **However, White People are hurt by racism in a different way.** I have talked about this often in workshops and when doing speaking engagements (and throughout this book).

We are socialized in ways that lead to distorted worldviews that shape our thinking, and behavior. The ideas that support racism are layered on top of this individual and collective dysfunction. It is the combination of foundationally distorted worldviews and the dehumanizing stereotypes and prototypes of ideological racism that create the lazy thinking and racially awkward interactions we experience. We are ill-equipped to navigate most relationships in a healthy way which is further compounded by ideological racism. In all cases, we default to self-centered and group-centered thinking at the expense of others: We take our own knowledge and other people's ignorance as givens. We assume that our way is necessarily other people's way. When we extrapolate from our own reality to what might be reality for others…we overreach.[5]

The interpersonal dynamics of racism are similar to a longstanding reciprocally codependent relationship. I am not diagnosing anyone because I am not a licensed anything. However, it doesn't take a clinical psychologist to see the relationship between the patterns and characteristics of codependency and interpersonal racism. How did I come to this conclusion? I came across a description about codependency in Steven Covey's book, *The 8th Habit* (pages 16 and 17):

> …People think that only those in positions of authority should decide what must be done. They have consented, perhaps unconsciously, to being controlled like a thing. Even if they perceive a need, they don't take the initiative to act. They wait to be told what to do by the person with the formal title, and then they respond as directed. Consequently, they blame the formal leader when things go wrong and give him or her the credit when things go well. And they are thanked for their "cooperation and support."
>
> This widespread reluctance to take initiative, to act independently, only fuels formal leaders' imperative to direct or manage their subordinates. This, they believe, is what they must do in order to get followers to act. And this cycle quickly escalates into codependency. Each party's weakness reinforces and ultimately justifies the other's behavior. The more a manager controls, the more he/she evokes behaviors that necessitate greater control or managing. The codependent culture that develops is eventually institutionalized to the point that no one takes responsibility. Over time, both leaders and followers confirm their roles in an unconscious pact. They disempower themselves by believing that others must change before their own circumstances can improve.
>
> The silent conspiracy is everywhere. Not many people are brave enough to even recognize it in themselves. Whenever they hear the idea, they instinctively look *outside* themselves…Perhaps you, too, are thinking that people who really need a book like this aren't reading it. That very thought reveals codependency. If you look at this material through the weaknesses of another, you disempower yourself and empower their weakness to continue to suck the initiative, energy and excitement from your life.[6]

As I read the passage, all I could see were the dynamics between White People and People of Color. We have internalized racism, reinforced it through interpersonal interactions, and institutionalized it to the point where no one takes responsibility; it is just a vicious cycle that we uphold. I also saw the connection to toxic, oppressive organizations that are conducive to racism-reinforcing interpersonal habits, among other habits that are harmful to our resilience. Although Covey uses the language of weakness to describe what we reinforce in each other, I see it as unhealthy, socialized patterns of behavior. What we are reinforcing in each another is the dysfunction that oppression and racism have facilitated within us on top of learned relationship dysfunction. Most of us did not one day wake up and agree to these terms; we were conditioned and the behaviors were normalized. Once I began to see these connections between codependency and racism, I needed to know more about codependency. So, I went down yet another rabbit hole of research.

A person who is codependent will plan their entire life around pleasing the other person (the enabler). In its simplest terms, a codependent relationship is when one person needs the other person, who in turn, needs to be needed. This circular relationship is the basis of what experts refer to when they describe the "cycle" of codependency.[7] The enabler's role is also dysfunctional. When we rely on a codependent, we do not learn how to have an equal, two-sided relationship and we often come to rely upon another person's sacrifices and neediness.

Codependency involves habits of unhealthy emotions, thinking, and behaviors in our relationships with others. It is a dysfunctional, one-sided relationship where one person relies on the other for meeting nearly all of their emotional and self-esteem needs. It also describes a relationship that enables another person to maintain their dysfunctional behavior. We are codependents when we have lost the connection to our core self, so that our thinking and behavior revolves around people and ideas external to us.[8]

I refer to the codependency of White People and People of Color as reciprocal, because the patterns can be seen within and across both groups. For example, there are times that internalized whiteness has People of Color seeking the attention and approval of White People to show that they are worthy and valuable because they are not like those *other* People of Color (also showing a codependency with other People of Color because we are seeing ourselves through their perceived weaknesses). In many cases, we are signaling our antiblackness by saying that we are not like those American Black People or African Americans (see Chapter 3).

Meanwhile White People do the same to People of Color to show that they are not like those *other* White People (also representing a codependency with other White People who are *the real racists*). In both instances we are seeking external validation of our humanity based on systemically reinforced ideas that infect us. Instead, energy can be more effectively put into holding up a mirror to ourselves to learn who we really are and how the world really works, developing our inner scorecard based on who we want to be, and building fulfilling relationships that are not transactional. We can opt out of being codependents to stop spending so much of our precious time stressing over situations and people over which we have no control. Instead, we can focus on our individual and collective growth and development.[8]

With codependency, the missing piece is a sense of separateness between our identities and other people's identities, known as emotional boundaries: Our thoughts and feelings belong to us and no one else is responsible for managing them. For real relationships to happen, we need to have a sense of our own identity and we need to feel safe enough to express our feelings without being afraid of criticism or rejection. As codependents we pursue each other, but never really develop a real connection, or we distance ourselves, but never really leave which creates constant pain in the relationship. Fleeting moments of closeness are just enough to keep some connection going, unless we give up on having a meaningful relationship. The alternative is to build our knowledge and skills to engage in healthy ones.

If you remember in the definition of a habit, addiction was present and includes activities. With racism being such a powerful collective habit, it is no wonder that there is such an uncanny parallel between the patterns of behavior usually attributed to addiction and the patterns of racial oppression. The fragmentation of our society shatters us as we are alienated and disconnected from our sense of self and each other.[9]

Then I wondered: How does codependency start? And the answer was particularly jarring to me. We are more likely to be codependents if:

- ⮑ We are taught that we are selfish if we want anything for ourselves; and as a result we learn to ignore our own needs and think only of what we can do for others at all times.
- ⮑ We are in the role of caregiver, especially at a young age, which may result in neglecting our own needs and developing a habit of only helping others.
- ⮑ We are abused; we learn to repress our feelings as a defense mechanism against the pain of abuse. This learned behavior results in caring only about another's feelings and not acknowledging our own needs.[7]

Selfish for wanting anything for ourselves: I began to remember a particularly antiblack sentiment that plays out all the time. When Black People, particularly African Americans, start organizing and advocating for themselves, everyone criticizes us that we are not being inclusive enough. However, every other race and ethnicity can organize and create infrastructure that focuses on their needs and issues. This communicates that Black People do not have the right to have our needs met and usually has a tone of suspicion because people have been conditioned to see us as angry, violent, and threatening. Or we are told to wait for some other issue that is more urgent to be addressed, so we need to be more patient and *eventually* our needs will be met.

In the role of caregiver: We constantly receive information that associates Black, Indigenous, and People of Color (BIPOC) with service providers and caregivers. These ideas, historical context, and policies have economically and socially locked BIPOC into caregiver roles for work, even in professional office settings when that is not their job (usually referred to as office housework). The types of businesses we own tend to reflect the same pattern of service-related industries which do not have very high profit margins.

Being abused: And finally, being BIPOC is a never-ending cycle of emotional (also referred to as psychological) abuse which involves scaring, humiliating, isolating, or ignoring people, as well as physical abuse.

As I read more about codependency, I also thought of Dr. Donna Hicks' book *Dignity*.[10] The framework of dignity she presents is the opposite of codependency; in fact her list of temptations to violate dignity align with the list patterns of codependency. Dr. Hicks defines dignity as "[t]he glue that holds all of our relationships together is the mutual recognition of the desire to be seen, heard, listened to, and treated fairly; to be recognized, understood, and to feel safe in the world."[11] At All Aces, we use the definition "To facilitate respect for our humanity by treating people and being treated as if we have value."

The traits of codependency are: Denial, Low Self-Esteem, Compliance, Avoidance, and Control. The table on the following page provides a high-level summary of these patterns of behavior. The content after the table is adapted from Co-Dependents Anonymous (yes, that is a thing) and elaborates on these concepts and their relationship to the dynamics of interpersonal racism. Whether intentional or not, the many thought leaders and researchers of internalized oppression have highlighted patterns of codependency between us and the ideas society attaches to us. After you review these traits of codependency, please remember to revisit the patterns of internalized oppression in the previous chapter.

Table 8: Codependency Patterns Adapted from PositivePsychology.com

Patterns of Codependency[12]		
	Unhealthy Patterns	**Alternative Healthy Patterns**
Denial	Denying, playing down, or misrepresenting our real feelings.	Owning and accepting our own emotions as valid and relevant.
	Lack empathy for the feelings and needs of others.	Feeling compassion for others - their emotions and human needs.
	Struggling to identify with/recognize our own feelings.	Self-awareness of own emotions. Being able to distinguish between thoughts and emotions.
Low Self-Esteem	Difficulty or inability to recognize/ask for things we want or require.	Being self-sufficient where possible, and seeking help, when appropriate, when it is needed.
	Struggling to establish adaptive boundaries with others.	Can set and maintain healthy personal boundaries.
	Holding other people's approval for our thoughts, emotions, and actions more highly than our own.	Self-confident. Respecting the opinions of trusted others without the need to 'win' approval.
Compliance	Neglecting or minimizing our own wants and needs to satisfy others.	Valuing our own wants and needs when others request something.
	Compromising personal beliefs and standards to avoid anger, disagreement, or rejection by others.	Upholding personal values and beliefs, even when they displease others.
	Trouble expressing own views, thoughts, and emotions when others' differ.	Respecting and suitably expressing our own personal beliefs and emotions, even when they differ from other people's.
Avoidance	Critically judging others' beliefs or actions.	Being accepting and open to others' opinions and beliefs.
	Repressing our own emotions and wants so that we do not feel vulnerable.	Trusting and esteeming our own emotions and needs, acknowledging and respecting our own vulnerability.
	Difficulty communicating when faced with potential confrontation or disagreement. Being evasive or indirect about conflict.	Expressing oneself clearly and in a straightforward way to resolve disagreements appropriately.
Control	Trying to persuade other people what to believe or do.	Being open and accepting about other people's views, decisions, and feelings, even when they differ from our own.
	Believing that others cannot look after themselves.	Appreciating that in most cases, mature adults can navigate their own issues.
	Insisting that other people fulfill their needs.	Seeking out resources to fulfil our own requirements, without asking it of others. Reaching out for help when necessary and appropriate without expecting it.

Denial. There are many reasons we use denial, including when we experience difficult emotions, have inner conflict, become comfortable with dysfunction (and therefore do not see it as a problem), or experience shame and trauma. When it comes to racism, BIPOC and White People have recurring moments of denial for many of these reasons. We are wired to deny as a survival mechanism. It is the first defense that we learn as a child. Denial of our experiences happens in four different degrees: [1] We refuse to believe that the problem, symptom, feeling or need exists. [2] We minimize or rationalize it. [3] We admit it exists but deny the impact or consequences. [4] We are unwilling to learn how to address the impact or get help.

Table 9: Denial Codependency & Interpersonal Racism

Denial Codependents	Healthy Thinking + Behavior
Have difficulty identifying what they are feeling.	We are aware of our feelings and identify them, often in the moment. We know the difference between our thoughts, feelings, and reality.
Minimize, alter, or deny how they truly feel.	We embrace our feelings; they are valid and important.
Perceive themselves as completely unselfish and dedicated to the well-being of others.	We know the difference between caring and care taking. We recognize that care taking for others is often motivated by a need to benefit ourselves.
Lack empathy for the feelings and needs of others.	We are able to feel compassion for another's feelings and needs.
Label others with their negative traits.	We acknowledge that we may own the negative traits we often perceive in others.
Think they can take care of themselves without any help from others.	We acknowledge that we sometimes need the help of others.
Mask pain in various ways such as anger, humor, or isolation.	We are aware of our painful feelings and express them appropriately.
Express negativity or aggression in indirect and passive ways.	We are able to express our feelings openly and directly, even when we are struggling with the weight of those emotions.
Do not recognize the unavailability of those people to whom they are attracted.	We pursue interactions and relationships only with others who want, and are able to engage in, healthy and meaningful relationships.

Low Self-Esteem. When we are low self-esteem codependents, we can be extremely insecure because codependents usually find a sense of meaning outside of themselves. Indecisiveness, overthinking, and poor communication skills are common. We look to others for approval and security. It takes a lot for us to feel comfortable admitting if we are wrong.

Personal boundaries are low, and we constantly question our words, actions, and appearance. We all have low self-esteem at times, but insecure codependents are different. Valuing other people's opinions above our own is a daily battle. We can struggle to feel an overall sense of peace and tend to harshly criticize ourselves and others. In a world where racism has added a layer of complexity to our existing dysfunction, BIPOC and White People can fall into this pattern as we reconcile our own identity versus what is constantly being communicated about who we are and how we are supposed to be, respectively. Much of the low-self-esteem-related codependency is in pursuit of an identity that we did not create for ourselves.

Table 10: Low Self-Esteem Codependency & Interpersonal Racism

Low Self-Esteem Codependents	Healthy Thinking + Behavior
Have difficulty making decisions.	We trust our ability to make effective decisions.
Judge what they think, say, or do harshly, as never good enough.	We accept ourselves as we are. We emphasize progress over perfection.
Are embarrassed to receive recognition, praise, or gifts.	We feel appropriately worthy of the recognition, praise, or gifts we receive.
Value others' approval of their thinking, feelings, and behavior over their own.	We value the opinions of those we trust, without needing to gain their approval. We have confidence in ourselves.
Do not perceive themselves as lovable or worthwhile persons.	We recognize ourselves as being lovable and valuable people.
Seek recognition and praise to overcome feeling less than.	We seek our own approval first and examine our motivations carefully when we seek approval from others.
Have difficulty admitting a mistake.	We continue to take our personal inventory, and when we are wrong, promptly admit it.
Need to appear to be right in the eyes of others and may even lie to look good.	We are honest with ourselves about our behaviors and motivations. We feel secure enough to admit mistakes to ourselves and others, and to hear their opinions without feeling threatened.
Are unable to identify or ask for what they need and want.	We meet our own needs and wants when possible. We reach out for help when it's necessary and appropriate.
Perceive themselves as superior to others.	We perceive ourselves as equal to others.
Look to others to provide their sense of safety.	We create safety for ourselves and advocate for others to respect it.

Low Self-Esteem Codependents	Healthy Thinking + Behavior
Have difficulty getting started, meeting deadlines, and completing projects.	We develop strategies to overcome the fear and uncertainty that leads to procrastination so we can meet our commitments in a timely manner.
Have trouble setting healthy priorities and boundaries.	We are able to establish and uphold healthy priorities and boundaries in our life.

Compliance. When we are compliant codependents, we almost always say "yes," and stay in unhealthy relationships. We also silence our own interests or desires to comply with someone else. We avoid change and therefore we tend to be "too loyal," including remaining in dangerous situations when we know it is not good for us. We tend to be extremely empathetic, meaning we sense and relate to the moods and feelings of others, but in a harmful way that can take on other people's feelings as our own. There is an underlying fear of rejection, and many live terrified of being "unworthy." We feel a need to ask permission before making decisions, and always worry if what we are saying is right. We never want to let others down, and often act too hard on ourselves if we make mistakes. As I wrote this, it reminded me of Malcolm X's description of the house negro:

> There were two kinds of slaves, the house Negro and the field Negro. The house Negroes--they lived in the house with master, they dressed pretty good, they ate good because they ate his food--what he left. They lived in the attic or the basement, but still they lived near their master; and they loved their master more than their master loved himself. They would give their life to save their master's house--quicker than the master would... If the master's house caught on fire, the house Negro would fight harder to put the blaze out than the master would. If the master got sick, the house Negro would say, "What's the matter, boss, we sick?" We sick! He identified himself with his master, more than his master identified with himself.

One major impact of this behavior is that we tend to confuse love with pity. As I mentioned in Chapter 4, pity is subtly expressed in a contemptuous, paternalistic, and self-centered way that is rooted in superiority. For BIPOC, there are White People in our lives who engage with us from a position of pity. This is the most common situation that I have observed. We are susceptible to confusing someone feeling sorry for us for really loving or appreciating us which can create a vicious cycle of codependency.

Table 11: Compliance Codependency & Interpersonal Racism

Compliance Codependents	Healthy Thinking + Behavior
Are extremely loyal, remaining in harmful situations too long.	We are committed to our safety and leave situations that feel unsafe or are inconsistent with our goals.
Compromise their own values and integrity to avoid rejection or anger.	We are rooted in our own values, even if others do not agree or become angry.
Put aside their own interests in order to do what others want.	We consider our interests and feelings when asked to participate in other people's plans.
Are hypervigilant regarding the feelings of others and take on those feelings.	We can separate our feelings from the feelings of others. We allow ourselves to experience our feelings and others to be responsible for their feelings.
Are afraid to express their beliefs, opinions, and feelings when they differ from those of others.	We respect our own opinions and feelings and express them appropriately.
Accept sexual attention when they want love.	Our sexuality is grounded in genuine intimacy and connection. We do not use it as a substitute for love.
Make decisions without regard to the consequences.	We consider possible consequences before we make decisions.
Give up their truth to gain the approval of others or to avoid change.	We stand in our truth and maintain our integrity, whether others approve or not, even if it means making difficult changes in our life.

Control. When we are controlling codependents, we need to be needed; our self-esteem depends on it. We believe other people cannot take care of themselves, and therefore, we need to be in charge of taking care of everyone else. We tend to give advice without being asked, blame or shame people around us for not being right, and feel resentful when others don't think or behave in ways we expect them to. Manipulation can be a huge sign of controlling codependents. Some of us can use charm or flirtation to get the approval we want from others. We tend to use manipulation and control as a way for those we are manipulating not to escape us. To feel valuable and useful we need others to continue to maintain their dependence on us, and we can only ensure this by controlling them. A common strategy to maintain someone's dependence is to undermine their self-esteem. If we make the other person feel worthless then they will need someone to come to their rescue. And that is when we save them, under the guise of being sacrificial.

BIPOC are oftentimes on the receiving end of this type of control codependency. We live in a society that has made conscious decisions to exclude BIPOC from its prosperity. Then the same society tinkers around the edges of BIPOC suffering to *save* us. We also see this behavior with BIPOC and White People who think they have all the answers to racism. They deem themselves the experts on racism based solely on being BIPOC or having read a book or attended a workshop. Then they inhumanely police everyone around them…fighting oppression with more oppression.

Table 12: Control Codependency & Interpersonal Racism

Control Codependents:	Healthy Thinking + Behavior
Believe people are incapable of taking care of themselves.	We realize that, with rare exceptions, other adults are capable of managing their own lives.
Attempt to convince others what to think, do, or feel.	We accept the thoughts, choices, and feelings of others, even though we may not be comfortable with them.
Freely offer advice and direction without being asked.	We give advice only when asked.
Become resentful when others decline their help or reject their advice.	We are content to see others take care of themselves.
Lavish gifts and favors on those they want to influence.	We carefully and honestly contemplate our motivations when preparing to give a gift.
Use sexual attention to gain approval and acceptance.	We embrace and celebrate our sexuality as evidence of our health and wholeness. We do not use it to gain the approval of others.
Have to feel needed in order to have a relationship with others.	We develop relationships with others based on mutual reinforcement, intimacy, and balance.
Demand that their needs be met by others.	We find and use resources that meet our needs without making demands on others. We ask for help when we need it, without expectations.
Use charm and charisma to convince others of their capacity to be caring and compassionate.	We behave authentically with others, allowing our caring and compassionate qualities to emerge naturally.
Use blame and shame to exploit others emotionally.	We ask directly for what we want and need. We do not try to manipulate outcomes with blame or shame.
Refuse to cooperate, compromise, or negotiate.	We cooperate, compromise, and negotiate with others in a way that honors our dignity and integrity.

Control Codependents:	Healthy Thinking + Behavior
Adopt an attitude of indifference, helplessness, authority, or rage to manipulate outcomes.	We treat others with respect and consideration
Use racial equity and social justice jargon in an attempt to control the behavior of others.	We use our racial equity and social justice knowledge for our own growth and not to manipulate or control others.
Pretend to agree with others to get what they want.	Our communication with others is authentic and truthful.

Avoidance. As avoidant codependents, we avoid conflict at all costs. Some of us may avoid intimacy as well. Usually, we appear to have a wall up and have a hard time expressing vulnerability. Distractions are tools that we use to avoid personal confrontation, as well as important life responsibilities, chores, or expressing gratitude and appreciation. Since avoidants fear conflict, they can often shut down when people around them are angry or upset. Another common trait of avoidant codependents is that they try desperately to get close to someone, only to then pull away with fear when a true bond begins to form. We try to avoid getting hurt more than anything.

Table 13: Avoidance Codependency & Interpersonal Racism

Avoidance Codependents:	Healthy Thinking + Behavior
Act in ways that invite others to reject, shame, or express anger toward them.to avoid closeness.	We act in ways that encourage loving and healthy responses from others without sacrificing ourselves.
Judge harshly what others think, say, or do.	We keep an open mind and accept others as they are.
Avoid emotional, physical, or sexual intimacy as a way to maintain distance.	We engage in emotional, physical, or sexual intimacy when it is healthy and appropriate for us.
Allow people, places, and things to distract them from achieving intimacy in relationships.	We practice our racial equity literacy and resilience to develop healthy and fulfilling relationships.
Use indirect or evasive communication to avoid conflict or confrontation.	We use direct and straightforward communication to resolve conflicts and deal appropriately with confrontations.
Diminish their capacity to have healthy relationships by declining to learn or use knowledge, skills, and tools.	When we use the tools of emotional intelligence and racial equity literacy, we are able to develop and maintain healthy relationships of our choosing.
Suppress their feelings or needs to avoid feeling vulnerable.	We embrace our own vulnerability by trusting and honoring our feelings and

Avoidance Codependents:	Healthy Thinking + Behavior
	needs.
Pull people toward them, but when others get close, push them away.	We welcome close relationships while maintaining healthy boundaries.
Sees themselves as solely responsible for their successes and as having control over others and things that they do not.	We understand that we are interconnected and interdependent with others and the world we live in.
Believe displays of emotion are a sign of weakness.	We honor our authentic emotions and share them when appropriate.
Withhold expressions of appreciation.	We freely engage in expressions of appreciation toward others.

All of the codependency and internalized oppression patterns listed align with several dignity violations framed by Dr. Donna Hicks:

- ➲ **Taking the Bait.** Do not take the bait of other people's bad behavior and use it to determine your own. Restraint is the better part of dignity. Do not justify getting even. Do not do unto others as they do unto you, if it will cause harm.
- ➲ **Saving Face.** Succumbing to the temptation to save face which includes lying, covering up, or deceiving ourselves. We need to tell the truth about what we feel and what we have done.
- ➲ **Shirking Responsibility.** Do not shirk responsibility when we have violated our own or others' dignity. We all need to admit when we have made a mistake and apologize for our impact on others, regardless of our intentions.
- ➲ **Seeking False Dignity.** Beware of the desire for external recognition in the form of approval and praise. If we depend on others alone for validation, we are seeking false dignity. Authentic dignity comes from building power within.
- ➲ **Seeking False Security.** Do not let your need for connection and relationship compromise your own dignity. If we remain in a relationship in which our dignity is routinely violated, our desire for connection has outweighed our need to maintain our own dignity. Resist the temptation to settle for false security.
- ➲ **Avoiding Conflict.** Stand up for yourself. It is essential that we do not avoid confrontation when our dignity is violated: We have to take action. A dignity violation is a signal that something in a relationship needs to change.
- ➲ **Being the Victim.** Assuming that we are the innocent victim in a troubled relationship. We need to be open to the idea that we might be contributing to the problem.

- ⮑ **Resisting Feedback and Help.** We often do not know what we don't know. We need to overcome our self-protective instincts and accept constructive criticism and support.
- ⮑ **Blaming and Shaming.** Blaming and shaming others to deflect our own guilt or responsibility in a situation is a dignity violation to ourselves and others. We are not being honest when we defend ourselves by making others look bad.
- ⮑ **Engaging in False Intimacy.** Beware of the tendency to connect by being critical and judgmental about others or trying to make people engage with us. If we want to create intimacy, we need to speak the truth about ourselves, about what is happening in our inner world, and invite the other person to do the same.

The types of racism-reinforcing and relationship-damaging ideas shaping our thinking and actions facilitate our dysfunctional interactions and relationships with each other. The fracturing of ourselves and our relationships damages our overall ability to build social capital. Social capital encompasses the skills and supports from direct personal relations, as well as the consequences of those relationships for access to economic, political and personal resources. One component of social capital is peer relationships. Researchers have identified different ways the layers of racism affect the development of both same-race and cross-race peer relationships.[13]

Peer relationships provide the context for us to develop the abilities and the catalyst to function well in a variety of personal and professional situations. Peers who are classmates or coworkers can support intellectual engagement, share knowledge and skills, and provide the social connections that create economic opportunity. Peers who are in personal relationships with us, such as friends, neighbors, and significant others, satisfy fundamental needs for belonging and can support the development of reimagined social norms and habits, including those necessary for physical and psychological health.[13]

Sticks & Stones

Words and how we frame things have meaning and consequences. Many thoughts we communicate to others carry logical fallacies that we are returning to the external world. These ideas and worldviews are based on our repeated exposure to, and internalization of, them, resulting in cognitive bias and cognitive distortions (see Chapter 3). I have added the Human Irrationality Process again in this chapter for your reference.

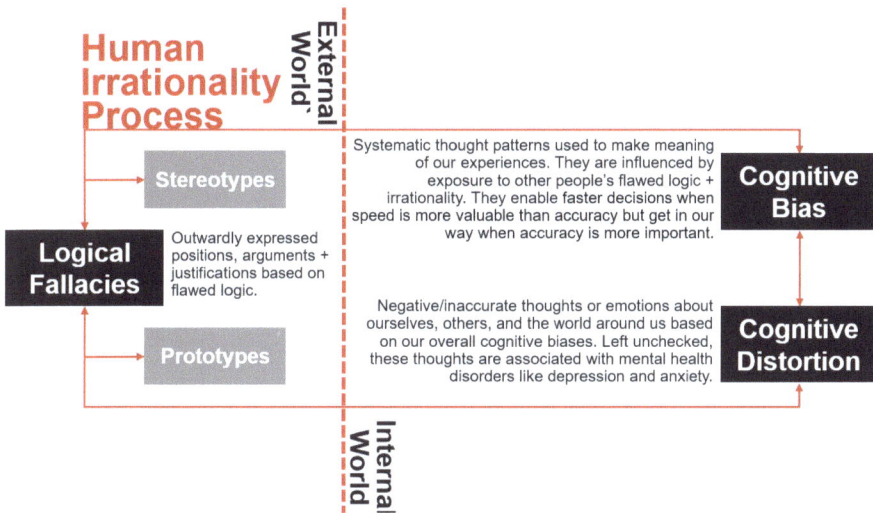

Figure 16: Human Irrationality Process (Overview)

In order to break the cycle of interacting with each other in ways that are counterproductive and reinforcing flawed thinking and oppression, we need to reimage our interactions. 'Power with' has to do with finding common ground among different interests and building collective strength. Based on mutual support, solidarity and collaboration, 'power with' multiplies individual talents and knowledge. 'Power with' can help build bridges across different interests to transform or reduce social conflict and promote equitable relationships and interactions. Advocacy groups that seek allies and build coalitions are drawing on the concept of 'power with'.

When we are in healthy relationships, we each feel fulfilled and at peace. If not, we know what to do to find personal fulfillment and can grow to accept ourselves in a healthy way. We can own up to our mistakes and shortcomings. Communication remains open, objective, and equally welcoming of each person's input and perspective. We are able to forgive each other and remain honest about personal life matters.

The satisfaction we can get from healthy relationships is strengthened by remembering there is no benefit in this short life to obsessing over trying to become validated by other people. We can politely say, "No" to people, situations, and demands that we do not feel comfortable with. Our life does not focus on trying to control others. We can be understanding to people in our lives without stressing over other their life decisions and making it about us.

By not focusing on others, but on ourselves, we develop a sense of capability within us to overcome personal challenges. Instead of feeling permanently stuck or victimized, we know we can figure out a solution in order to move forward in life. We are able to recognize damaging behavior and feel confident to stand up for ourselves when someone continually treats us or others poorly. We are willing to leave a toxic relationship if it puts us or our family in any harm.

Healthy Debates

There are tools that can help us identify the approaches we are using when we argue or debate. The following is an adaptation of Paul Graham's "Hierarchy of Argumentation." It is a tool that can help navigate verbal conflict to clarify our position and the positions of others. It allows us to use different strategies and tactics to raise the sophistication of our positions on issues and learn to respond to others in productive ways. This visual of Graham's "Hierarchy of Argumentation" describes each level and how it relates to conversations.

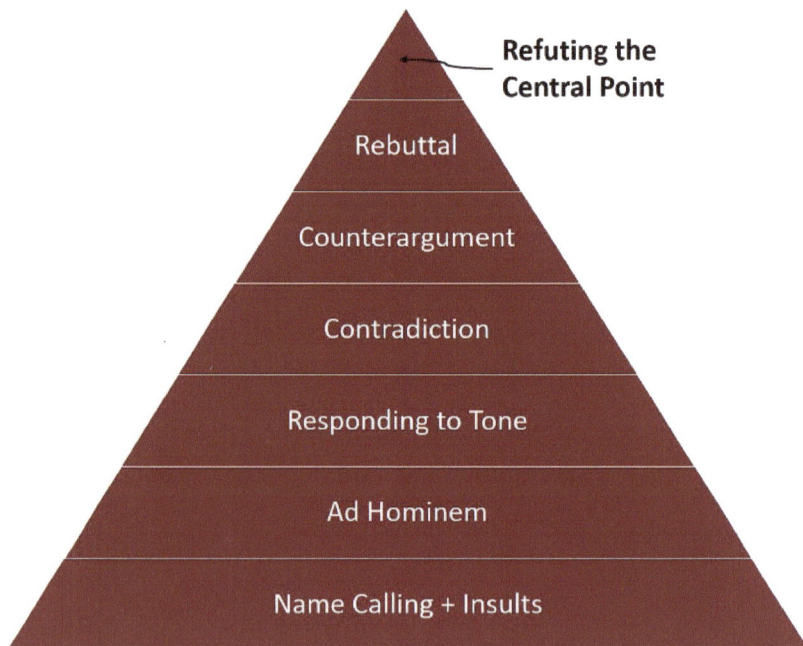

Refuting the Central Point

Rebuttal

Counterargument

Contradiction

Responding to Tone

Ad Hominem

Name Calling + Insults

Figure 17: Graham's Hierarchy of Argumentation

Name Calling + Insults: This is the lowest form of disagreement, and also the most common. There is no actual argument, just negative emotions represented as adjectives intended to hurt another person. This includes calling BIPOC radical, socialists, angry, aggressive, unprofessional, or that the accuser feels threatened based on nothing but our discomfort and stereotypes. It is also easy to take the bait or lead with name calling towards

White People. Just as our humanity as BIPOC needs to be preserved, so does the humanity of White People with whom we are communicating.

Ad Hominem. An ad hominem attack is not quite as weak as mere name-calling. It might actually carry some weight. It may not address the topic or argument at hand but may be relevant to the case. Regardless, it is still a very weak form of disagreement. Saying that someone lacks the authority to discuss an issue or topic is also a type of ad hominem—and a particularly useless type, because good ideas often come from outsiders. The question is whether the person is correct or not. If this lack of authority caused someone to make mistakes in their logic, then we should point those out. And if it did not, it is not relevant.

Responding to Tone. At this level we start to see responses to the argument, rather than the person. However, disagreeing with the tone is not a sophisticated approach. It matters much more whether the person's position is rational than how they said it. Tone is very hard to judge and if the worst thing we can say about someone's position is to criticize the tone, we are not saying much. If someone is incorrect in their position, say exactly where. This is a hard one. There are emotions associated with engaging in difficult conversations that can be expressed in a way that makes it hard to hear what people are saying. I see this most often when BIPOC are advocating and White People are offended that BIPOC have emotions and are frustrated. Do not police the tone of other people. Usually when we are discussing tone with BIPOC, it is because we are uncomfortable with the reality that went unnoticed mixed with paternalism. BIPOC we also have an opportunity to be better in policing other people's tone as that is not the central issue we are trying to work towards (people can change their tone and still reinforce racism).

Contradiction. This is the first level where we finally get responses to what was actually said, rather than how or by whom. However, the lowest form of response to an argument is simply to state the opposing case, with little or no supporting evidence. It is often combined with the previous levels of arguments, but with limited substance and quality. Contradiction can sometimes have some weight. Sometimes merely seeing the opposing case stated explicitly is enough to see that it is right. But usually evidence will help.

Counterargument. At this level we reach the first form of convincing disagreement: counterargument. Counterargument might prove something. The problem is, it is hard to say exactly what. Counterargument is contradiction plus reasoning and/or evidence. When aimed squarely at the original argument, it can be convincing. But unfortunately, it is common for counterarguments to be aimed at something slightly different. More often than not, two people arguing passionately are arguing about two different things. Sometimes they even agree with one another but are so caught up in their squabble they do not realize it. There could be a legitimate reason for arguing against something slightly different from what the other person said: when you feel they missed the heart of the matter. But when you do that, you should say explicitly that that is what you are doing.

Rebuttal. The most convincing form of disagreement is refutation. It is also the rarest because it is the most work. Indeed, the disagreement hierarchy forms a kind of pyramid, in the sense that the higher you go the fewer instances you find. To refute someone it is helpful to quote them or restate their point. We have to find a "smoking gun," a specific statement in whatever we disagree with that we feel is mistaken, and then explain why. If we cannot find an actual statement to disagree with, we may be arguing with a straw man (against a point they were not making). While refutation generally entails quoting, they are not one and the same. Some writers quote parts of things they disagree with to give the appearance of legitimate refutation, then follow with a response at a lower level of argument.

Refuting the Central Point. The force of a refutation depends on what you refute. The most powerful form of disagreement is to refute someone's central point. Even at this highest level of argumentation we still sometimes see deliberate dishonesty, as when someone picks out minor points of an argument to refute. Sometimes the spirit in which this is done makes it more of a sophisticated form of ad hominem. For example, correcting someone's grammar, or harping on minor mistakes in names or numbers. Unless the opposing argument depends on such things, the only purpose of correcting them is to discredit our opponent. Truly refuting something requires a critique of its central point, or at least one of them. And that means one has to commit explicitly to what the central point is. The quotation you point out as mistaken need not be the actual statement of the author's main point. It is enough to refute something it depends upon.

When We Are Under Fire

Criticism and feedback can deplete our self-esteem if we let it. However, it can be a blessing in disguise. We readily criticize others because we can observe their behavior. However, it is very difficult to observe our own behavior or be aware of how it impacts other people. Feedback becomes an important consideration in our own development and growth. However, most of us fear it (it is the first cousin of conflict). I was reading an oldie but goodie, *Feeling Good*, by Dr. David Burns, which provides clinically proven drug-free treatment for depression. I have found it to be a great book that is helpful for anyone to read. There was a section in the book called *Verbal Judo* and I perked up (I am a mixed martial artist (MMA) fan…yes, that is a part of me too). Judo techniques are generally intended to turn an opponent's force to one's own advantage rather than to oppose it directly.

Step One: Empathy. Ask the person a series of specific questions to find out exactly what they mean. Here is the most important and difficult part: Avoid being judgmental or defensive as you ask the clarifying questions. Constantly ask for more specific information to increase your ability to see the world through the critic's eyes. Some people will default to the lowest level of Graham's Hierarchy of Argumentation (see previous section), name calling insults, or ad hominem attacks. Your questions are meant to guide them to a higher level of argument so you can understand the situation. For many people, this part of the process will derail their attempt to cause you harm if the intention of their feedback is not to be helpful. If they are trying to be helpful, empathy will shift or prevent the dynamics from being an attack-defense interaction to one of collaboration and mutual respect.

Step Two: Disarming the Critic. Do not run from or get on the defensive. Stay engaged and disarm the person. Regardless of whether the person is right or wrong, initially, find some way to agree with them; even if they are making criticisms of you that you feel are unfair, not valid, or unrealistic. You can agree in principle with the criticism, you can find some grain of truth in the statement and agree with that, or you can acknowledge that the person's feedback or feelings are understandable because it is based on how they experienced the situation. The goal is to find some way to agree with whatever the person says, avoid sarcasm or defensiveness, and always speak the truth. Avoiding defensiveness is particularly significant because if we give in to our default tendency, the intensity of the negativity and attack increases. At this point, if the person is still worked up, they will usually calm down.

Step Three: Feedback and Negotiation. Now that we have listened to the other person with empathy and disarmed them with agreement, now you will be able to explain your position tactfully but assertively, and to negotiate any real differences. If the person is completely wrong (based on facts), you can express this in a developmental way. Express your perspective objectively and acknowledge that you might be wrong. This helps us to avoid our own self-centeredness or pride for a more rational approach. Remember that the person's mistake does not make them stupid, worthless, or inferior. It makes them human, just like you. By staying developmental and non-defensive, it allows us and the people we interact with to avoid a confrontation that threatens our self-respect and dignity. In the same vein, if you were mistaken in the situation, thank the person for providing you the information, and apologize for any hurt or harm you may have caused.

Hopefully more people will learn these skills and we may be fortunate enough to experience someone extending this kind of grace to us when we are mistaken with our feedback or criticism for another person.

Disruptors of Interpersonal Racism: Elevate Abundance + Engage to Learn + Embrace Discomfort + Collective Care

"Those who authentically commit themselves to the people must re-examine themselves constantly."[14] – Paolo Freire

Our ability to manage ourselves and our relationships are intricately connected. For our own sake, we need to learn how to forgive others for their flaws and faults because we are flawed as well. We have all been guilty of not being empathetic towards other people. The degree that we can empathize with another human being is directly related to our ability to empathize with ourselves, which is another way internalized oppression influences interpersonal interactions. Our ability to empathize with others expands our personal capacity for growth and to have empathy for ourselves.

For particularly toxic people, we may struggle to forgive them. However, we still do not have to allow them to drive our emotions and therefore our thinking and behavior. We can let them keep their poisonous ways of being and not allow ourselves to be poisoned in the process by living in the moments when we were bitten.

When we engage with each other as human beings, both the person communicating and the person receiving information have distortions. Racism's influence on how we see ourselves and others is a consistently powerful distortion of each other's humanity. The process of working through these distortions is what leads to authentic interactions.

The habits of racism in interpersonal interactions are fairly predictable. Therefore, they lend themselves to practicing how we will respond in those moments to avoid trying to make it up on the spot under pressure. How will you create the space you need to form a response that matches the moment and helps you accomplish what you need to get done? Thinking about it ahead of time lessens the shock. We may experience some surprise, but we do not have to be shaken by racism and just react…we can have a response.

The following approaches for disruptors of oppression are built upon the social competence aspect of emotional intelligence. Social competence is an area of emotional intelligence that focuses on social awareness and relationship management. To be aware of others and how we are impacting them requires us to develop some level of personal competency in emotional intelligence that includes self-awareness and self-management. Additionally, conflict management as well as *intra*personal + *inter*personal communication skills. We can create unique personal and professional interactions by making the ordinary extraordinary, seeking to understand the meaning of the moment, and building courage in ourselves and other people.[15]

Elevate Abundance. We can work with other people to structure win/win relationships focused on results so we can establish meaningful, effective relationships that foster mutuality, belonging, and progress. If we standardize cooperation, we can establish a standard of an abundance mentality that realizes there are lots of opportunities that we can collectively tap into by problem-solving how to ensure everyone gets what they need. This process of collective thinking and action requires us to build trust by investing in relationships and finding shared values and doing authentic acts of kindness. This process also includes establishing clear agreements on collaborating with each other and following through on our commitments. Finally, we can align our personal and organizational habits to support opportunities to reinforce the creation of win-win outcomes.

Engage to Learn. We listen to other people to understand their feelings and the meaning they are trying to communicate before seeking understanding for ourselves.[16, 17] If we maintain a healthy ego and put aside defensiveness, we can invest in meaningful dialogue, relationships, and outcomes. The follow is a set of recommendations for conversations that are difficult or crucial:[17, 18]

- ⮑ **Recognize Your Story**: Identify how the specific issues, impact, assumptions, and identities influence the narrative we created before a conversation.
- ⮑ **Make it Safe to Speak**: Be clear about our emotions and thoughts, embrace mutual purpose, and offer mutual respect.
- ⮑ **Proactively Listen**: Manage our inner conversation, listen for meaning and emotion, and clarify what we heard.
- ⮑ **Speak Honestly & Carefully**: Express feelings with courage tempered by consideration for the feelings of others.

Embrace Discomfort. When we embrace discomfort, we welcome diverse perspectives, problem solving, and work through conflict and mistakes. This creates new, exciting, and unexpected discoveries that were not possible working alone or only working with people or on issues we are most comfortable.

- ⮑ **Seek & Respect Diversity**: Actively look for diverse people and perspectives inside and outside your usual networks or your organization to problem-solve
- ⮑ **Prepare for Problems**: Create a process to mitigate, respond to, and recover from interpersonal issues and organizational trauma
- ⮑ **Learn from Problems**: Explore process, systemic, and cultural problems or failures to learn how to inform ways to prepare for

future issues

➲ **Address Root Causes**: Resist scapegoating other people who surface legitimate problems; instead, look to find and address the root causes of the issues being surfaced.

Dealing with ourselves is hard enough. Then we have to learn how to deal with ourselves while also navigating other people. This chapter provided context on why it is so hard and some strategies to learn and practice to see what works for you. In the next chapter, we will explore how the ideas we have internalized not only impact the way we interact with one another interpersonally, but how we structure and operate organizations.

Chapter 5. Interpersonal: The Daily Routines of Racism

1.   Chae DH, Nuru-Jeter AM, Adler NE, et al. Discrimination, racial bias, and telomere length in African-American men. *American Journal of Preventative Medicine*. Feb 2014;46(2):103-11. doi:10.1016/j.amepre.2013.10.020

2.   Chae DH, Epel ES, Nuru-Jeter AM, et al. Discrimination, mental health, and leukocyte telomere length among African American men. *Psychoneuroendocrinology*. 2016;63:10-16. doi:http://dx.doi.org/10.1016/j.psyneuen.2015.09.001

3.   Glasberg SD, Shannon D. *Political Sociology: Oppression, Resistance, and the State*. Pine Forge, an Imprint of Sage Publications; 2011.

4.   Williams P. *Seeing a Color-Blind Future: The Paradox of Race*. The Noonday Press; 1997.

5.   Buckingham M, Goodall A. The Feedback Fallacy. Harvard Business Review. March-April 2019 ed2019.

6.   Covey SR. *The 8th Habit: From Effectiveness to Greatness*. Free Press a Division of Simon & Shuster, Inc.; 2004.

7.   Berry J. What's to know about codependent relationships? Medical News Today. Accessed 11/14/2020, https://www.medicalnewstoday.com/articles/319873

8.   Lancer D. Problems of Codependents. Psych Central. Accessed 11/10/2020, https://psychcentral.com/lib/problems-of-codependents/

9.   Alexander BK. Healing Addiction through Community: A Much Longer Road Than it Seems? https://www.brucekalexander.com/articles-speeches/treatmentarecovery/286-healing-addiction-through-community-a-much-longer-road-than-it-seems-2

10.   Hicks D. *Dignity: Its Essential Role in Resolving Conflict*. 2011.

11.   Hicks D. What Is the Real Meaning of Dignity? Few people realize its extraordinary impact on our lives. Psychology Today. Accessed 11/11/2020, https://www.psychologytoday.com/us/blog/dignity/201304/what-is-the-real-meaning-dignity-0

12.   PositivePsychology.com. Shifting Codependency Patterns. Accessed 11/9/2020, https://positivepsychology.com/codependency-definition-signs-worksheets/

13.   Brondolo E, Libretti M, Rivera L, Walsemann KM. Racism and social capital: The implications for social and physical well-being. *Journal of Social Issues*. 2012;68(2):358-384. doi:10.1111/j.1540-4560.2012.01752.x

14.   Freire P. *Pedagogy of the Oppressed*. Bloomsbury; 1970:183.

15.   Heath C, Heath D. *The Power of Moments: Why Certain Experiences Have Extraordinary Impact*. Simon & Schuster; 2017.

16.   Covey SR. *7 Habits of Highly Effective People: Powerful Lessons in*

Personal Change. Simon & Schuster; 2013.

17. Patterson K, Grenny J, McMillan R, Switzler A. *Crucial Conversations: Tools For Talking When Stakes Are High.* Second ed. McGraw-Hill; 2012.

18. Stone D, Patton B, Heen S. *Difficult Conversations: How to Discuss What Matters Most.* 10th Anniversary ed. Penguin Books; 1999.

6. INSTITUTIONAL: THE BIGGEST REWARDS

"Working on a problem reduces the fear of it. It's hard to fear a problem when you are making progress on it – even if progress is imperfect and slow. Action relieves anxiety." – James Clear, 3-2-1 Thursday Newsletter (9/24/2020)

Most organizations have built a culture that operates as if when racism happens, it is random. We tell ourselves and others, "It is just one bad apple" or "racism has no place here, we do not tolerate it." Racism is not random…it is systemic and systematic. It is everywhere, predictable, and explainable AND there is a broad landscape of action available to us to catalyze and sustain a Diversity, Inclusion, and Equity Transformation (DIET).

Part of the challenge we face is that institutional racism sits on top of existing organizational dysfunction, just like the other layers of racism are amplified by our personal dysfunction. When an organization does not have an intentionally developed culture, it defaults to mimicking society's unhealthy, habitual attitudes and behaviors. The unchecked social habits we bring to organizations are detrimental to employees' and the organization's ability to reach their full potential.

I have shared this reality in front of many audiences around the world: As I mentioned before, my husband and I have five children, two still at home. We have struggled over the years to find a way to inoculate our children from being infected with whiteness as an ideal and anti-Black stereotypes and sentiments. These seeds of objectification easily cultivate preprogrammed default settings of whiteness that create a false sense of self for Black, Indigenous, and People of Color (BIPOC) and White People. However, we have learned the power of having an intentional family culture that nurtures our children's resilience, sense of self, and their perceptions of possibilities in their lives. We had to break the chain of societal and historical dysfunction and irrational conformity that fuels racism.

What does my family's journey have to do with organizations? It is the first time I consciously understood what culture really is, how it works, and its power. But what is culture? In an organization, just like my family, culture is the collective of values, accountability, and practices that guide and inform every aspect of *how* an organization accomplishes its mission and works towards its vision.

Organizational Habits of Racism

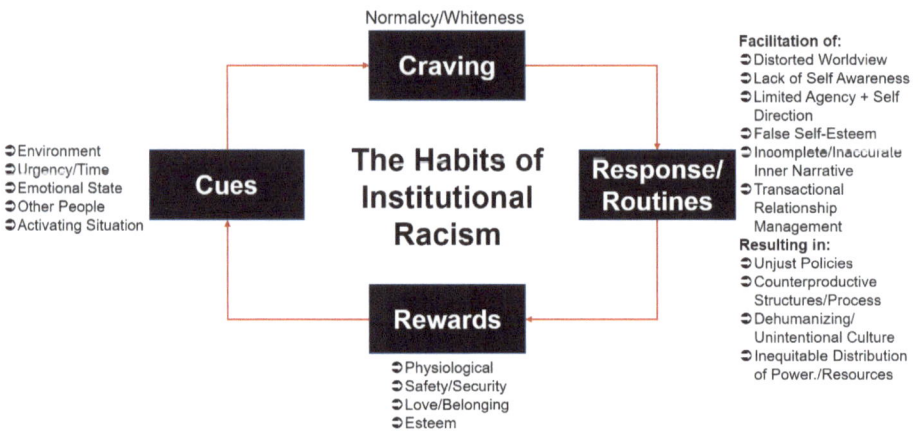

Normalcy/Whiteness

Craving

Cues

The Habits of Institutional Racism

Response/Routines

Rewards

➲Environment
➲Urgency/Time
➲Emotional State
➲Other People
➲Activating Situation

➲Physiological
➲Safety/Security
➲Love/Belonging
➲Esteem

Facilitation of:
➲Distorted Worldview
➲Lack of Self Awareness
➲Limited Agency + Self Direction
➲False Self-Esteem
➲Incomplete/Inaccurate Inner Narrative
➲Transactional Relationship Management
Resulting in:
➲Unjust Policies
➲Counterproductive Structures/Process
➲Dehumanizing/ Unintentional Culture
➲Inequitable Distribution of Power./Resources

Figure 18: Organizational Habits of Racism

Organizations have the opportunity to create cultures of belonging that explicitly confront its own contributions to racism and create a roadmap to racial equity. Every organization in America has permeable barriers where whiteness and antiblackness seep in to shape the habits that dictate what gets done and how. As such, there has to be a restructuring of organizational culture that is jointly created with everyone and challenges everyone to amplify the experiences and realities of BIPOC in the process. As mentioned in Chapter 2, the same illogical and destructive ideas of whiteness that embed themselves into organizations are harmful to BIPOC and White People. The experiences of BIPOC in an organization are symptoms of larger organizational structure, process, and culture issues.

Organizations, much like families, have the power to set the conditions for breaking the chain of conformity and wastefulness. The more disruptive an environment is to oppression, the less likely our individual implicit racial bias will manifest in our behavior.[1, 2] Although policies (written and unwritten) are important, they are only one part of a meaningful strategy. Culture shift requires more than a policy, it requires clarity on: Who are we as an organization (current state of affairs/organizational sense of self)? Who do we want to be (mission, vision, values)? What needs to change so we can all move in the direction towards our best organizational/collective selves? What are our priorities (informed by who we want to be)? What will the barriers be (so we do not use them as an excuse)?

In the previous chapter I mentioned how rereading Stephen Covey's 8th Habit inspired me to explore codependency. The following is the passage again because in the context of institutional racism, it takes on a different context:

> …People think that only those in positions of authority should decide what must be done. They have consented, perhaps unconsciously, to being controlled like a thing. Even if they perceive a need, they don't take the initiative to act. They wait to be told what to do by the person with the formal title, and then they respond as directed. Consequently, they blame the formal leader when things go wrong and give him or her the credit when things go well. And they are thanked for their "cooperation and support."
>
> This widespread reluctance to take initiative, to act independently, only fuels formal leaders' imperative to direct or manage their subordinates. This, they believe, is what they must do in order to get followers to act. And this cycle quickly escalates into codependency. Each party's weakness reinforces and ultimately justifies the other's behavior. The more a manager controls, the more he/she evokes behaviors that necessitate greater control or managing. The codependent culture that develops is eventually institutionalized to the point that no one takes responsibility. Over time, both leaders and followers confirm their roles in an unconscious pact. They disempower themselves by believing that others must change before their own circumstances can improve.
>
> The silent conspiracy is everywhere. Not many people are brave enough to even recognize it in themselves. Whenever they hear the idea, they instinctively look *outside* themselves…Perhaps you, too, are thinking that people who really need a book like this aren't reading it. That very thought reveals codependency. If you look at this material through the weaknesses of another, you disempower yourself and empower their weakness to continue to suck the initiative, energy and excitement from your life.[3]

I added the passage in this chapter because the dynamic described between positional leaders and employees is a pattern that organizations facilitate resulting in oppressive environments. And when we layer the codependency dynamics of racism on top of the positional leader and employee codependency, it is a stew of social and organizational "hot messness" (in other words a steaming mess of constant chaos and dysfunction).

Black, Indigenous, and People of Color (BIPOC) are often not acknowledged, seen, or heard in organizations, with elected officials, and other spaces of traditional power. It is not because we do not try, but because people work to ignore and silence us. Our advocacy makes other people uncomfortable, so we become the problem instead of the real problems we are surfacing. In fact, the issues surfaced are harmful to others beyond BIPOC because they represent the broken places of an organization, systems, and our country. The oppressive dynamics of minimizing, silencing, and gaslighting are playing out in organizations across the country where BIPOC are fighting for their return on investment, in many cases, alongside White accomplices. BIPOC tolerate dignity violations because we need to meet our underlying needs. We need to meet our deficiency needs: feed our families, have stability, feel like we belong, and respect ourselves and be respected by others. These are the same needs White People have. However, because of organizational dysfunction and racism, we barely have our basic needs considered, let alone our growth needs.

As a country, we have increasingly been discussing the disproportionate burden of America's structural and systemic problems on BIPOC, especially Black People. Despite growing awareness, we still exhibit the same thinking and behavior that leads to these perverse outcomes. These recurrent missteps are the signs and symbols of policy, practice, and culture challenges that disproportionately harm BIPOC, while also negatively impacting White People.

Diversity, Equity, Inclusion + Sometimes Justice

There is a constant evolution of language in the fields of racial equity, antiracism, social justice, Diversity, Equity, and Inclusion (DEI), Diversity and Inclusion (D&I), and Justice, Equity, Diversity, and Inclusion (JEDI). The range of ways we refer to the work reflects the challenges of keeping up.

We need to understand the way oppression works and how it applies to our lives and organizations. This knowledge then allows us to see more opportunities for action as disruptors of racism and oppression. Knowing the definitions of words is a key building block to learning but meaning is about how the concept relates to things we already understand about the world, how it relates to our own experiences and context, and what it means to our individual and collective behavior (I am focusing on the context of advancing racial equity). Then we can apply the concept to different situations and put it practice in our lives and organizations.[4]

For the purpose of reframing how we think about this work in organizations, I am advocating for a Diversity, Inclusion, and Equity Transformation (DIET) for organizations.

Power. Organizations with unintentional culture tend to operate from a place of 'power over.' 'Power over' is the most commonly recognized form of power. It has a lot of negative associations for many of us, such as repression, force, coercion, discrimination, corruption, and abuse. Power is seen as a win-lose relationship. Having power involves taking it from someone else, and then using it to dominate and prevent others from gaining it. In politics, those who control resources and decision-making have power over those without. When people are denied access to important resources like land, healthcare, and jobs, 'power over' perpetuates inequality, injustice and poverty.

Hidden forms of power are consciously and unconsciously used by people who benefit to maintain their power and privilege by creating barriers to participation, by excluding key issues from the agenda, or by controlling decision making and resource distribution behind the scenes or behind closed doors. They may occur not only within political processes, but in organizational and other group contexts as well, such as workplaces, NGOs, coalitions, or community-based organizations. BIPOC can reinforce these systems without realizing it, because of the threat to our livelihoods or we benefit at the detriment of other BIPOC, even if we do not consciously take these positions.

Through hidden forms of power, alternative choices to the status quo are limited, people without traditional power and their concerns are excluded, and the rules of the game are set to be biased against BIPOC and the issues most impacting them. Academics have described this form of power as the 'mobilization of bias', where 'some issues are organized into the agenda or narrative while others are organized out'.[5] This is done by seemingly rigid rules and procedures (some people have relationships and influence to go around), the framing of issues in a way that devalues them, the uses or threat of sanctions, and the discrediting of the legitimacy of people who challenge the status quo.

Strategies that address this form of power focus on strengthening people's voices and capacities to speak out, mobilizing and organizing to overcome the barriers to participation, using research and media to challenge how issues are framed. Often when we talk about hidden power, we talk about how people affected negatively by power may challenge it, to make their voices more visible. Leadership should expect to see overt and covert resistance and advocacy as people gain their voice, especially if organizations continue to ignore the way racism and other forms of oppression impact employees, clients, communities, etc.

This tension of short-term versus long-term plays out in racism all the time. We are so busy trying to get work done in organizations, passing legislation, etc. that we refer to efforts that can advance racial equity as something that can be dealt with another time. The urgency creates a false dichotomy and reinforces all-or-nothing thinking. It is false because *how* we do our work needs to embed racial equity. It is not an extracurricular activity. The investment now can have long-term benefits for our lives, communities, organizations, and larger society. Racial Equity and DEI are not extracurricular activities, they are practices that need to permeate impact every aspect of our organizations.

Why So Much Resistance to Diversity, Equity, and Inclusion Efforts?

"The most difficult thing for individuals to do when they're part of the team is to sacrifice. It's so easy to become selfish in a team environment… Willing sacrifice is the great paradox. You must give up something in the immediate present – comfort, ease, recognition, quick rewards – to attract something even better in the future; a full heart and sense that you did something which counted. Without sacrifice, you'll never know your team's potential, or your own." – Pat Riley

Researchers have found five maladaptive defense mechanisms related to behavioral intention to resist organizational change: projection, acting out, isolation of affect, dissociation and denial.[6] Projection had the strongest association with behavioral intentions to resist change compared to other unhealthy defense mechanisms. Our mind tricks us into believing that the cause of the anxiety towards the change is located in somebody else. In other words, we unconsciously and falsely attribute our own unacceptable feelings, impulses, and thoughts to others. We see in others what is really inside of us and tend to put blame on them instead of accepting our own faults, flaws, and inner conflict. What is really an internal threat is now believed to be external.

If we are trying to make changes to advance racial equity (or any other kind of change for that matter) we have to stop following the easy path of technical approaches that try to avoid the human dynamics that will be present whether we acknowledge them or not.[7] Since organizations consist ultimately of people, organizational change essentially involves personal change.[6] When we are implementing change, leadership needs to be aware of how human thinking and behavior, such as irrational ideas and emotion, may influence how people respond to that change. We need to implement intervention strategies and techniques that start with creating self-awareness and then develop processes to minimize irrational thoughts. Our personal growth and development is likely to alter our perceptions of change which reduces the level of resistance to organizational change.[8] However, there may be legitimate reasons there is resistance. This is why voice and choice are so important (I will come back to this shortly).

The volume of literature on behavior analysis may contribute to creating more effective nudges. As discussed in Chapter 2, nudges are environmental or situational cues that influence our decisions with the goal of steering people towards *better* decisions. However, there are ethical debates about the legitimacy of behavior control: Who controls the controllers? We as people (all of us) have blind-spot biases and failing to recognize our biases is a bias in itself – it is called naïve realism when we think that we see the world around us objectively and that people who disagree with us must be uninformed, irrational, or biased.[9] Future research on the contact point of nudging and behavior analysis is needed to elaborate on these ethical considerations. After all, behavior control and paternalism represent two faces of the same coin, a coin that play a central role in behavior analysis and nudging.[10]

In order to increase the success of DEI or racial equity efforts, we need to involve employees in the development, implementation, and evaluation processes. Voice, choice, and accountability are critical ingredients to advancing racial equity and liberation of our full potential. The combination of these ingredients as well as professional and personal development has the benefits of: (1) delegitimizing the acceptance of whiteness and antiblackness as an automatic entitlement to privileges; (2) decreasing the likelihood of escape or avoidance from responsibility for harm; (3) unlocking creativity, diligence, and problem solving; and (4) increasing the likelihood that people are more resilient to change and challenges in the organization.

Modern views of motivation focus on it as a time-linked set of repetitive and reciprocating emotional, behavioral, and cognitive processes and actions that are organized around our goals. Our goals (the mental representation of a desired outcome) do not exist in isolation but rather within a complicated network of continuous processes at the intersection of nature, nurture, and the situations we encounter.[11] So when our goals do not seem to align with the organization's, there is conflict. And once again, conflict is healthy if we learn and employ conflict management skills to gain clarity on where we all stand on an issue and what is important to us.

Voice and choice are the other reasons DEI and racial equity efforts fail. The very people responsible for doing the work are not involved in the process. It is yet another paradox: We are working towards creating organizational environments that are not oppressive by perpetuating oppression. As Paolo Freire said "…to alienate human beings from their own decision-making is to change them into objects." Now, I never thought I would do this, but I am affirming Freire's quote with a Stephen Covey quote: "…many in positions of authority do not see the true worth and potential of their people and do not possess a complete, accurate understanding of human nature, *they manage people as they do things*."[3] The first step in rehumanizing leadership approaches is to make decisions *with* employees instead of for them.

Accountability is the willingness to accept responsibility for our individual, collective, and organizational actions. When individuals and organizations are accountable, we understand and accept the consequences of our actions. Without accountability, the change process breaks down quickly. When it does, people externalize the need to change, resist initiatives designed to move them forward and even sabotage efforts to transform the organization. With accountability, people at every level of the organization embrace their role in facilitating the change and demonstrate the ownership needed for making true progress, both for themselves and their organization. Accountability, done the right way, produces greater transparency and openness, enhanced teamwork and trust, effective communication and dialogue, thorough execution and follow-through, sharper clarity and a tighter focus on results.[12] This is hard work and it is human nature to want to quit when things get difficult . However, it is working through the adversity of the journey that we get the greatest gains for our organizational journey.[13]

Healing is in the Doing. Many leaders in organizations often have a default desire to heal through dialogue. Dialogue is an important component of reconciling. However, it is a vehicle to a destination that everyone needs to be clear about. Healing is an output of decisive action to address the wounds and learning how to prevent those wounds from happening again. This requires developing and implementing a much larger racial equity vision and mission.

Black, Indigenous, and People of Color (BIPOC) and White People who care are tired of the avalanche of words without a subsequent avalanche of resources and action. In order to take meaningful action, we need to build the capabilities of leaders and teams to create the kind of organization they want to be a part of. When we think of a business or a government agency, we think in terms of boxes, arrows, and charts, not people. But organizations ARE people (not in the corporate sense): They are the sum of the people in them and the policies and practices they create and uphold.[8]

The Need for an Organizational Diversity, Inclusion, and Equity Transformation [DIET]: Equity Opportunities

DIVERSITY, INCLUSION, & EQUITY TRANSFORMATION (DIET) FRAMEWORK ©				
All Aces, Inc. CONDUCIVE →				DISRUPTIVE
EQUITY OPPORTUNITIES	INCREASING LEVELS OF ORGANIZATIONAL DEVELOPMENT →			
STRATEGIC DIRECTION	Unaware or uninterested in how racism and other forms of oppression impact the organization's mission, functions, culture, and staff. Has no policies or practices in place and justifies doing things the way they've always been done.	Accepts the existence of racism and other forms of oppression but only does the minimum required by law, collects basic data, and some policies are developed but the responsibility sits with a limited few such as Human Resources or a committee.	Includes specific language in vision and/or mission related to racial equity and social justice as well as develops metrics that are tracked and communicated across the organization to address racism and other forms of oppression.	Integrates addressing racism and other forms of oppression into all policies and practices to reflect and reinforce strategic direction while also actively supporting and tapping into all employees, ensuring people of color and other marginalized groups are meaningfully engaged.	Demonstrates leadership, innovation, and courage in challenging racism and other forms of oppression within field/industry while creating space in its operations for consciousness, critical thinking, and a commitment to continuous personal, professional, and organizational improvement.
STRUCTURE & PROCESS					
NORMS & STANDARDS					
COMMUNICATION					
KNOWLEDGE					
RELATIONSHIPS					
DECISIONMAKING					
RESOURCES					

Figure 19: Diversity, Inclusion, and Equity Transformation (DIET) Framework

Organizations that create the conditions for an environment disruptive to oppression increase the likelihood that people will be able to think and behave as disruptors of oppression. The following Equity Opportunities from the DIET Framework provide an overview of the practical approaches we can take to transform our organizations into resilient places where people and the organization can thrive. I will provide an overview of the equity opportunities (landscape of action) in the DIET Organizational Framework.

Communication, knowledge (building and sharing), and relationships are the core equity opportunities for organizations to develop because they facilitate their ability to address structural, process, and culture challenges. They are important for organizations because of how the layers of racism and other forms of oppression overlap and influence one another. An organization's ability to support employees in developing these skills helps people to work through how racism-reinforcing ideas can manipulate us in how we think about ourselves and other people (internalized racism) and engage each other (interpersonal racism). Additionally, they inform how the organization can strengthen all equity opportunities.

Communication. All aspects of communication come together in an organization. Our ability to individually and organizationally express thoughts and feelings with courage, tempered by consideration for the thoughts and feelings of others, impacts everything we do. Communication and the flow of information throughout the organization can facilitate or hinder equity. The same approaches to intrapersonal and interpersonal communication in Chapter 5 are foundationally important. The flow of information through the organization is impacted by our level of proficiency in personal communication and considerations for the variety of realities within the organization.

Knowledge Building. Knowledge building is the ability of an organization to gather, synthesize, and process information and experiences to create a robust shared pool of meaning. If we are doing authentic employee and stakeholder engagement, it supports other equity opportunities, especially decision making. We have enough information to make quality decisions, even when the circumstances do not facilitate our ability to have a more collaborative process in the moment. We create space to understand knowledge about racial equity and experiences of underestimated groups that are not being contributed to the organizational narrative. Understanding the range of stories people tell about the organization, their experiences, and their observations provides a rich source of information that can inform decision-making. When we keep our finger on the pulse, we have better context to make decisions when time pressures or other limitations make it hard to engage in a collaborative process.

Relationships. Relationships are the engine that facilitates how effectively and efficiently the work that supports an organization's mission happens. It is also a documented critical component of the employee experience.[14] Development of formal and informal social capital built on trust, collaboration, and conflict management helps us feel a sense of belonging. We can analyze how the other building blocks of organizational culture/equity opportunities impact conditions that facilitate relationships.

Relationships are built on trust and, as you have probably heard before, relationships, productivity, and processes move at the speed of trust. Yes, this is another Stephen Covey reference,[3, 15] but he is not the only one to discuss this. The first of only two women to win the Nobel Prize in economy, Elinor Ostrom, co-edited a book of research articles that examine the role of trust in relationships and sharing resources.[16] In Figure 32, I have integrated the considerations for trust and the DIET Framework (which aligns with the components of the research Ostrom led – mainly because the DIET Framework is based on standard organizational/group development components).

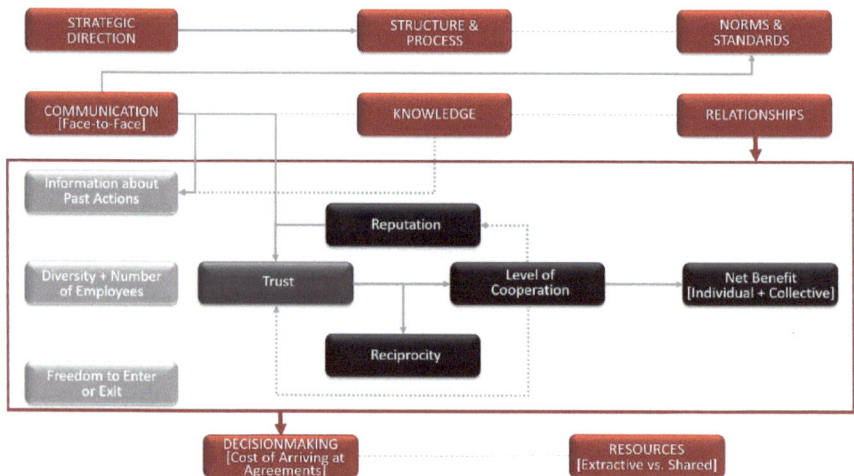

Figure 20: Importance of DIET Core Equity Opportunities to Organizational Development (Partially Inspired by the Book Trust & Reciprocity)

Strategic Direction. The vision, mission, values/principles, and goals of an organization make up the strategic direction. Collectively, we can revisit existing strategic language to determine if the strategic direction communicates the organization's commitment to racial equity; and/or if it is clear to stakeholders internally and externally how the strategic direction facilitates equity.

The first place to start with any transformation is changing our collective consciousness. To shift our strategic direction, we need to know where we stand by conducting an organizational assessment. There is a need to ensure that the findings inform rather than replace action. Just because an organization is committed to being a diverse and equitable organization does not necessarily mean that they are.[17]

Norms and Standards. An organization's norms and standards represent its practiced values in the form of habits. The goal is to determine if the habits of an organization align with the stated values in its strategic language and its commitment to equity and belonging. Ultimately, we are what we do on regular basis. Our practiced values should not be different from our stated ones. This applies to our professional, personal, and organizational actions. We often try to squeeze time and energy into racial equity or DEI efforts in isolation of how we behave and do our jobs. If we are not being honest about where we are collectively as an organization AND integrate our strategic direction with our norms and standards (what we actually do), then we are not going to close the gap between the two.[18]

Structure and Process. Structure and process includes an organization's leadership style, hierarchy, policies, tools, workflow, and individual/organizational evaluation process. They present opportunities to identify how the organizational composition and business flow facilitate or act as barriers to equity and belonging.

Leaders have the biggest impact on the direction of the organization. Businesses, nonprofits, and government can only progress as far as the development of leadership. Organizational transformation is a function of leadership's developmental stage (see Chapter 1).[19] The most transformative leaders have a process to manage their thinking,[20] build meaningful relationships,[21] and coach people into finding and keeping their own voice.[22]

In the absence of alternative models and relationships, many of us repeat the 'power over' pattern in our personal relationships, communities and institutions. This is also true for those of us who are Black, Indigenous, and People of Color. When we as BIPOC gain power in leadership positions, we oftentimes imitate what we think leadership looks like, which is based on oppressive concepts and dehumanized approaches. For this reason, we cannot expect that the experience of being excluded prepares us to become democratic leaders. New forms of leadership and decision-making must be explicitly defined, taught, and rewarded in order to promote more democratic forms of power.

"The only realm in which humans are an unimpeachable source of truth is that of their own feelings and experiences…Humans are unreliable raters of other humans."[23] This statement from a Harvard Business Review article has huge implications for people in organizations, especially BIPOC and other marginalized people. It suggests that the current approach to providing feedback is flawed because we offer it through the lens of our own expectations and things that are helpful to our development. However, we do need developmental feedback to better see ourselves through the experiences of others we encounter, because most of us are not walking around with a mirror held up to ourselves to see when we make mistakes or have unproductive habits. When leaders learn and use a coaching approach, they help invest in the development of employees with meaningful guidance that is intrinsically driven and not from external perceptions and attempts to motivate or change people. As discussed in the previous chapter, to fully benefit from feedback we need humility to own our impact, and a strong sense of self to discern which feedback is valuable.

Decision-making. Decision-making is the process of making choices by identifying a decision to be made, gathering information, and assessing alternative choices while managing our ego and distorted automatic thoughts. The goal is to have organizational processes that are transparent, accountable, uses appropriate tools, and, ultimately, are equitable. There is no one-size-fits-all way to make decisions. However, there are important considerations that facilitate trust and collaboration. The first consideration is to be clear about where the decision-making authority lies:

- ⮑ Who has the authority to make specific types of decision — which individual, team, or department?
- ⮑ What is the maximum appropriate involvement of employees and/or other key stakeholders in any decision made?
- ⮑ Which decision-making method is most appropriate given the situation?
- ⮑ Is the decision-making method and the reasons for it transparent?

We are all faced with bounded rationality, the idea that our ability to be rational is limited by: (1) the time available or urgency (the time pressure or importance of the decision – including potential impact on others in the organization), (2) the complexity of the issue (which likely requires more context, information, and/or collaboration), and (3) our cognitive capacity (which is influenced by biases, tiredness, stress, ego functioning, etc.).[24] This reality of our humanity leads to decisions that are status quo instead of optimal. However, we can learn how to recognize and leverage these data points to inform which decision-making approach we need to take within an organization (this also applies to individuals).[25]

Resources. Resources are the combination of people, finances, space, time, and other assets that express the (mis)alignment of the stated strategic direction versus actual organizational investments. This not only applies to racial equity, but to everything else in an organization. If you want to know what the priorities of an organization are, look at how it spends its money and time.

Time is such an important and undervalued resource. In addition to monitoring how our workplaces use time, we also need to pay attention to how BIPOC are expected to spend time and how they are rewarded. In many organizations, BIPOC are expect to be a part of all the DEI efforts. However, they oftentimes do not receive any professional or career credit for the additional work those commitments bring.

Instead of trying to set aside extracurricular time and energy to *work on*

DEI or racial equity, we need to invest many types of resources into integrating it into how we accomplish our mission and live our values. Resources act as an input into, an output from, and an outcome of shifting from the habits of racism to co-created habits for racial equity.

If you are interested in learning more about each of these equity opportunities in the DIET Framework, please join IntentionallyAct.com for free access. In the final chapter, I will review the big picture and share an example from my most recent leadership experience.

6. Institutional: The Biggest Rewards

1.   Ziegert JC, Hanges PJ. Employment discrimination: the role of implicit attitudes, motivation, and a climate for racial bias. *Journal of Applied Psychology.* May 2005;90(3):553-62. doi:10.1037/0021-9010.90.3.553

2.   Brief AP, Dietz J, Cohen RR, Pugh SD, Vaslow JB. Just Doing Business: Modern Racism and Obedience to Authority as Explanations for Employment Discrimination. *Organizational Behavior and Human Decision Processes.* 2000/01/01/ 2000;81(1):72-97. doi:https://doi.org/10.1006/obhd.1999.2867

3.   Covey SR. *The 8th Habit: From Effectiveness to Greatness.* Free Press a Division of Simon & Shuster, Inc.; 2004.

4.   Brown PC, Roediger HL, McDaniel MA. *Make It Stick: The Science of Successful Learning.* The Belknap Press of Harvard University Press; 2014.

5.   Schattschneider E, E. *The Semisovereign People: A Realist's View of Democracy in America.* Harcourt Brace College Publishers; 1960.

6.   Bovey WH, Hede A. Resistance to organisational change: the role of defence mechanisms. *Journal of Managerial Psychology.* 2001;16(7):534-548. doi:10.1108/eum0000000006166

7.   Kotter JP, Cohen DS. *The Heart of Change: Real-Life Stories of How People Change Their Organization.* Harvard Business Review Press; 2002.

8.   Bovey WH, Hede A. Resistance to organizational change: the role of cognitive and affective processes. *Leadership & Organization Development Journal.* 2001;22(8):372-382. doi:10.1108/01437730110410099

9.   Tavris C, Aronson E. *Mistakes Were Made (But Not by Me): Why We Justify Foolish Beliefs, Bad Decisions and Hurtful Acts.* Houghton Mifflin Harcourt Publishing Company; 2015.

10.   Simon C, Tagliabue M. Feeding the behavioral revolution: Contributions of behavior analysis to nudging and vice versa. *Journal of Behavioral Economics for Policy.* 2018;2(1):91-97.

11.   Kanfer R, Chen G. Motivation in organizational behavior: History, advances and prospects. *Organizational Behavior and Human Decision Processes.* 2016;136:6-19. doi:10.1016/j.obhdp.2016.06.002

12.   Connors R, Smith T. *Change the Culture, Change the Game: The Breakthrough Strategy for Energizing Your Organization and Creating Accountability for Results.* Penguin Group; 2011.

13.   Godin S. *The Dip: A Little Book That Teaches You When to Quit (and When to Stick).* 2007.

14.   Harter JK, Schmidt FL, Agrawal S, Plowman SK, Blue A. *The Relationship Between Engagement at Work and Organizational Outcomes: 2016 Q12® Meta-Analysis.* 2019. https://news.gallup.com/reports/257567/gallup-q12-meta-analysis-report.aspx

15.   Covey SR. *7 Habits of Highly Effective People: Powerful Lessons in Personal Change*. Simon & Schuster; 2013.

16.   *Trust and Reciprocity: Interdisciplinary Lessons for Experimental Research.* The Russell Sage Foundation Series on Trust. Russell Sage Foundation; 2003:424.

17.   Trenerry B, Paradies Y. Organizational Assessment: An Overlooked Approach to Managing Diversity and Addressing racism in the Workplace. *Journal of Diversity Management*. 2012;7(1):11-26.

18.   Kotter JP, Cohen DS. *The Heart of Change: Real-Life Stories of How People Change Their Organizations*. Harvard Business Review Press; 2012.

19.   Rooke D, Torbert W. Organizational transformation as a function of CEO's developmental stage. *Organizational Development Journal*. 1998;16(1):11-28.

20.   Garvey Berger J. *Unlocking Leadership Mindtraps: How to Thrive in Complexity*. Standford Briefs, an Imprint of Stanford University Press; 2019.

21.   Sinek S. *Leaders Eat Last: Why Some Teams Pull Together and Others Don't*. Penguin Business; 2019.

22.   Bungay Stanier M. *The Coaching Habit: Say Less, Ask More & Change the Way You Lead Forever*. Box of Crayons Press; 2016.

23.   Buckingham M, Goodall A. The Feedback Fallacy. Harvard Business Review. March-April 2019 ed2019.

24.   Wheeler G. Bounded Rationality. In: Zalta EN, editor. The Stanford Encyclopedia of of Philosophy. Fall 2020 ed: Stanford University; 2018.

25.   Buchanan L, O'Connell A. A Brief History of Decision Making. *Harvard Business Review*. 2006;(January 2006)

7. THE HABITS OF RACIAL EQUITY

An intentional practice to re-humanize and reinforce the power of People of Color and White People not based on whiteness, but our shared humanity and different realities. The ideology of individual and collective power and humanity is embedded in internalized, interpersonal, and institutional habits that facilitate People of Color and White People reaching their full human potential. – All Aces, Inc.

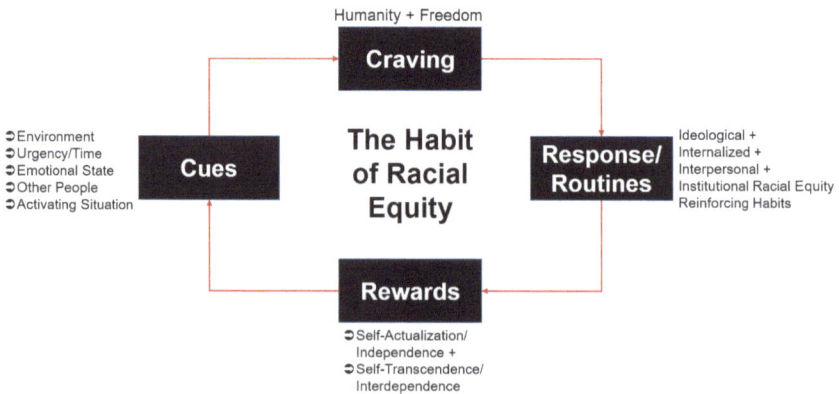

Humanity + Freedom

Craving

⊃Environment
⊃Urgency/Time
⊃Emotional State
⊃Other People
⊃Activating Situation

Cues

The Habit of Racial Equity

Response/ Routines

Ideological +
Internalized +
Interpersonal +
Institutional Racial Equity
Reinforcing Habits

Rewards

⊃Self-Actualization/
Independence +
⊃Self-Transcendence/
Interdependence

Figure 21: The Habit of Racial Equity

As the Chief Resilience Officer for the City of Boston under Mayor Martin J. Walsh, I brought many racism and racial equity lessons and experiences into city hall. I continued to intently learn and revisit resources that provided context on what racism is, how it works, how it impacts us as individuals and in organizations, and approaches to address it from the social justice and racism-specific literature (books, reports, peer-reviewed articles, videos, etc.). Over the years, it seemed like many of these resources were missing major pieces of the puzzle, but I could not put my finger on what was missing. However, I began to see a pattern: Racism seemed to exist at the intersection of neuroscience, sociology, and psychology. After going down rabbit holes of learning about implicit bias; critical thinking; habit formation and change; individual, organizational, and community trauma; human and organizational development; cognitive behavioral therapy; behavioral economics; leadership; and more, I decided that throughout the entire process of the resilience strategy, we would model a different way for local government to be which included embedding racial equity.

During my tenure as Chief Resilience Officer, we engaged the community in a way that local government usually does not. I created a collaborative approach to framing the problems and our strategy which involved over 100 stakeholders (community residents, community organizations, government, and businesses) who were called the Boston Resilience Collaborative. They steered the direction of the work throughout the research and writing process.

We conducted community engagement by riding buses and trains in areas that were predominantly BIPOC to capture the concerns and ideas of the people who did not have the time privilege to attend other types of engagement we were doing (community meetings, music festivals, plays, movie screenings, etc.). A tiny office whose staff never reached four members – with the help of interns, fellows, and the Boston Resilience Collaborative – reached over 12,000 residents in Boston. We started with the issue of racism, proposed a strategy with specific actions and supported it with research that was community-based and engaged.

I share this story because I represented a bureaucratic system of organizations that, at the time, was not known for innovations in confronting racism within a city with a reputation for being one of the most racist in the country. Through incorporating voice and choice throughout the process and allowing myself and the city to be held accountable to that, we developed a strategy that received international attention (which was not the goal). We were able to produce such a meaningful strategy because we had a collaborative process with a clear vision, values, and shared learning.

The process I have described was very difficult: I experienced interpersonal and institutional racism along the way. There were roadblocks to sustaining a substantive focus on the layers of racism. However, I am so proud of all of the people who sacrificed their precious time to participate in the Boston Resilience Collaborative and who engaged with us at events and on public transportation. It was such a special few years that it kept me going through the medical challenges I was dealing with - which were so severe that other people with the condition have taken a year or more of professional leave.

I have had similar experiences throughout my career, including when I was the director of the Office of Public Health Preparedness for Boston's local public health department. I was responsible for leading the emergency management planning process across all of the public health and healthcare infrastructure in Boston (the health department, hospitals, community health centers, pharmacies, home care, nursing homes, and more). We also developed partnerships with community organizations working with residents who were predominantly BIPOC or serving residents who were living in poverty (including the working poor). The planning process required to develop this response infrastructure across so many stakeholders required significant collaboration, and creative but realistic, problem solving.

When emergencies happened, I had to lead the process of putting those plans into play by activating our Stephen M. Lawlor Medical Intelligence Center (MIC). The MIC is the physical location where public health and healthcare partners come together to coordinate situational awareness, resources, and human services. In addition to supporting traditional public health and healthcare partners, we sanitized sensitive information from situation reports about emergencies so we could keep our community partners updated.

I happened to be in this role when the Boston Marathon Bombings happened. We had the MIC activated as part of standard Boston Marathon protocols (the city used the marathon as a way to test our emergency management systems). What is not often mentioned in any mainstream discourse on the bombings is the significant coordination across public health and healthcare as well as mental health and trauma response practitioners. There were unimaginable amounts of resource and information coordination in the first few months as well as direct support provided to survivors for two years.

What is never mentioned is the increase in gun violence in Boston in the ensuing months after the bombings. In addition to the traditional emergency of the bombings, our BIPOC communities were dealing with this increase shootings as a real community emergency. Our team began to feel the impacts of this reality when we started getting requests for psychological trauma response resources from community partners that were not associated with the bombings, but shootings. We created a process to ensure we were able to deploy teams to support BIPOC communities. The Boston Marathon Bombings was on full international display as Boston Strong. However, we did not take that same type of care and resource investment in BIPOC communities' pain and suffering.

My team and I met (a lot) with community organizations to create a whole set of protocols for leveraging MIC infrastructure and apply it to community emergencies like shootings and other traumatic events that impacted large numbers of community members. Through this process, we also developed a network of community partners to be a part of the response. We fought for resources to compensate community organizations. We treated them like the experts and partners that they were.

I originally did not plan on sharing anything about the bombings in this book. It is still a whirlwind of superlative negative and positive emotions and memories. However, I thought it was an important example of a tale of two cities. Sharing this story is an opportunity to show that even in the midst of disaster, racial equity and social justice can be embedded. I think at some point, I will write more on it since there is so little known about this aspect of the Boston Marathon Bombings response. I do not know when I will be ready for that, so in the meantime, I will add some content on IntentionallyAct.com.

Collaborative processes that respect the humanity of people engaged and stay focused on the mission, yield results that far exceed what a small group can achieve in a silo. We need the range of context from those closest to the issues because they live them, study them, and care about them. When racial equity and social justice is embedded in the process, the output is significantly more impactful. It means that we are intentional about avoiding the traps that come with our human condition and the layers of racism. We will produce in a way that is less likely to perpetuate racial inequities, other social injustices, and oppressive conditions.

Is it easy? No. Is it doable? Yes. Can you do it? Yes. Adopting approaches that are disruptive to oppression take more work and challenge us more…just like true democracy does. However, it is what creates transformative change, fulfilling experiences, and saves time on the back end - we do not need to spend so much valuable time defending ill-informed decisions and strategies if we have a truly collaborative process that embeds racial justice. The rewards we get from more equitable approaches should address the deficit needs (food, belonging, etc.) of those involved while also creating experiences that support growth needs – helping people expand and leverage their power within (overcoming invisible power) and power to (agency/autonomy) and engaging in power with or collective action (see Chapter 2). Doing the right thing takes more work. However, overcoming the struggle to fall into status quo traps facilitates special experiences and outcomes that draw others to us and our organizations.[1, 2]

Now that I have transitioned to building and growing my own business, I have been able to create a number of frameworks, tools, and strategies to develop and apply the knowledge and skills discussed in this book. As the CEO and founder of All Aces, Inc., I have had the pleasure of designing a mission- and values-driven business that uses a personal, professional, and organizational development approach to catalyzing transformative change in organizations for racial and social justice. I decided that I would create the kind of organization that I wish I could have worked in…one that anyone focused on growth needs would want to be. I am so proud of Team All Aces for living our values every day, no matter how hard it is.

We use an evidence- and experience-informed, applied-learning approach that is about knowledge and skills-building. Then we facilitate a process that allows people to apply their learning and skills to developing and implementing strategies that shift culture, structure, and process.

The figure below provides a summary of the theory of change that Team All Aces uses to help ourselves and our clients take meaningful, strategic action to transform. It should be familiar to you if you have read the previous chapter up to this point (and did not skip around like I do when I first open a book to determine if I am going to read the whole thing).

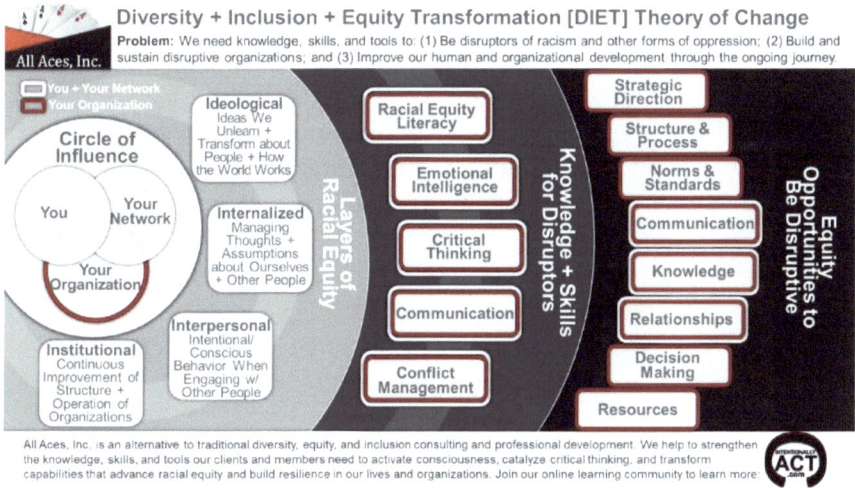

Figure 22: All Aces' DIET Theory of Change

The following section provides an overview of the professional and personal (PROPER) development journey that builds the knowledge and skills for disruptors and creates the foundation for organizations to leverage equity opportunities to be disruptive.

Disruptors of Racism: Developmental Approach to Resilience + Racial Equity [DARRE] Model

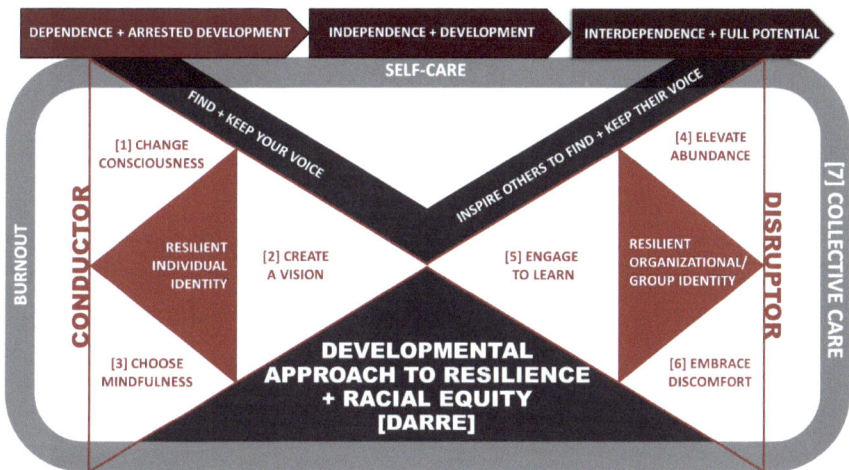

Figure 23: Developmental Approach to Resilience + Racial Equity

[1] Change Consciousness

The first step in any change process, individual or organizational, is to learn and reframe our perspective on what we are trying to change. This means we must learn about why we think and behave in ways that habitually support the limitations racism and other forms of oppression have placed on our identities.

Changing our consciousness allows us to build knowledge that clarifies our conductor/disruptor roles as individuals and organizations, how it plays out in society, and our opportunities to choose new ways of thinking and behaving.

Learning Objectives

- ⮑ Connect Social Context: Evaluate our current racial realities by exploring how psychology, neuroscience, and sociology influence our development, and the types of thinking and behavior that reinforce oppressive conditions
- ⮑ Explore Historical Context: Connect our collective racial history to present-day inequities, especially the specific historical context that impacts your life, community, and industry
- ⮑ Internalize Lessons: Identify our own underlying beliefs and habits that contribute to the system of racism
- ⮑ Examine Strategies + Tools: Explore promising resources for changing our individual and organizational habits/practices.

[2] Create a Vision

Creating a vision is about developing a clear image of what it means to be a proactive disruptor of racism and to have a proactively disruptive organizational culture. This includes building the resilience necessary to sustain our efforts. It also includes identifying our vision, values, and goals for ourselves and our organizations that reflect who and how we would like to be on our racial equity journey.

Learning Objectives

- ⮑ Develop a Vision and Values: Decide on who and how we

would like to be and how we want our organizations to run

⮑ Reflect on Internalized Lessons: Prioritize our previously identified list of habits that passively conduct racism

⮑ Identify Goals: Choose specific actions that help us turn our vision and values into a reality

⮑ Commit to Strategies + Tools: Determine which resources will help us remove obstacles to fulfilling our full potential.

[3] Choose Mindfulness

Choosing mindfulness is about making the changes necessary for our desired vision and goals through new personal and organizational habits that create conditions disruptive to oppression. It requires us to align our lives and organizations to facilitate adopting the behaviors to reach our vision and goals.

Learning Objectives

⮑ Establish a Routine: Integrate mindfulness techniques and new habits into current healthy habits

⮑ Remove Barriers: Identity friction to our commitment within our environment and reduce them

⮑ Join a Community: Align with people who already have the habits we are seeking to build [IntentionallyAct.com is a good place to start]

⮑ Reflect and Review: Remain mindful of our progress over time through journaling, self-talk, organizationally facilitated employee and stakeholder engagement, etc.

[4] Elevate Abundance

Elevating abundance helps us to work with other people to structure win/win relationships focused on abundance. It means that we do the hard work of establishing meaningful, effective relationships that foster mutuality, belonging, and progress.

Learning Objectives

⮑ Standardize Cooperation: Establish a standard of an abundance mentality which realizes there are lots of opportunities that we can collectively achieve instead of individually competing with each other

- ➲ Build Trust: Invest in building trust in relationships with colleagues by finding shared values and acts of kindness
- ➲ Honor Commitments: Establish clear agreements on collaborating with colleagues, follow through on those commitments, and hold each other accountable for doing the same with you/your team/organization
- ➲ Align Systems + Processes: Adjust the supporting equity opportunities in the DIET Framework (e.g. structure and process, decision making, resources) to reinforce the creation of win/win outcomes.

[5] Engage to Learn

Engaging to learn means that we listen to other people to understand their feelings and the meaning they are trying to communicate to us before seeking understanding for ourselves. This requires us to maintain a healthy ego and put aside defensiveness to invest in meaningful dialogue, relationships, and outcomes.

Learning Objectives

- ➲ Recognize Your Story: Identify how the specific issues, assumptions, and identities impact the narrative we create before a conversation
- ➲ Make it Safe to Speak: Be clear about your emotions and thoughts, embrace mutual purpose, and offer mutual respect.
- ➲ Proactively Listen: Manage our inner conversation, listen for meaning and emotion, and clarify what we heard
- ➲ Speak Honestly & Carefully: Expressing feelings with courage tempered by consideration for the feelings of others

[6] Embrace Discomfort

Embracing discomfort is about welcoming diverse perspectives, problem solving, and working through conflict and mistakes. This helps us to uncover new, exciting, and unexpected discoveries that were not possible working alone or only working with people or on issues we are most comfortable.

Learning Objectives
- ➲ Seek & Respect Diversity: Actively look for diverse people and perspectives beyond our usual social circles and professional networks
- ➲ Prepare for Problems: Create a process to mitigate, respond to, and recover from interpersonal challenges and organizational trauma (this is not about compliance-based, risk mitigation structures we currently have)
- ➲ Learn from Problems: Explore process, systemic, and cultural problems to learn how to inform preparation for future issues
- ➲ Address Root Causes: Resist scapegoating individuals who surface issues instead, address the root causes of the issues they are surfacing.

[7] Collective Care

Collective care creates the space for people to continuously develop and take care of themselves and each other. It fuels our resilience so we can sustain individual and organizational progress towards racial equity and more humanized approaches.

Learning Objectives
- ➲ Facilitate Learning: Provide opportunities to continue to increase skills for knowledge building and sharing, communication, and relationships
- ➲ Support Renewal: Create the time and financial resources to help people take care of themselves in the ways that are helpful to them (sometimes this means people learning what that means; there is no singular practice for everyone)
- ➲ Collective Care Culture: Look for ways to implement time and space in the supporting equity opportunities of the DIET Framework to reinforce core equity opportunities: knowledge building and sharing, communication, and relationships.

It is my sincerest hope that you have found something in this book that is helpful on your personal or organizational journey. Please remember to embrace calculated risk and avoid blindly following someone else's template for living, leading, and loving.

Chapter 7. The Habits of Racial Equity

1.   Heath C, Heath D. *The Power of Moments: Why Certain Experiences Have Extraordinary Impact.* Simon & Schuster; 2017.
2.   Godin S. *The Dip: A Little Book That Teaches You When to Quit (and When to Stick).* 2007.

ABOUT THE AUTHOR

Dr. Atyia Martin is the CEO and Founder of All Aces, Inc., an alternative to traditional diversity, equity, and inclusion consulting and professional development. Instead, All Aces is a Racial Equity Applied Learning [REAL] Partner with a mission to activate consciousness, catalyze critical thinking, and transform capabilities that advance racial equity and build resilience. They offer practical professional, personal, and organizational development which includes their online learning community, IntentionallyAct.com. Additionally, Dr. Martin is a Distinguished Senior Fellow at Northeastern University's Global Resilience Institute. She has over 20 years of experience in resilience, applied learning, social and organizational equity, emergency management, public health, and intelligence.

As a certified emergency manager, her previous professional roles include Chief Resilience Officer for the City of Boston, director of the Office of Public Health Preparedness at the Boston Public Health Commission, and adjunct faculty in the Master of Homeland Security and Public Policy programs at Northeastern University. Dr. Martin has also held positions at the Boston Police Department's Boston Regional Intelligence Center; City of Boston's Mayor's Office of Emergency Management; the Federal Bureau of Investigations (FBI); the Air Force as active duty assigned to the National Security Agency; and the Initiative for a Competitive Inner City.

Dr. Martin and her husband were born and raised in Boston where they currently live. They co-founded Next Leadership Development Corporation, a nonprofit focused on building resilience in Black households and communities. They have five children, two still at home.

www.ingramcontent.com/pod-product-compliance
Lightning Source LLC
Chambersburg PA
CBHW040130270326
41928CB00001B/12